THE BEST
100
CAKES

THE BEST
100
CAKES

A fabulous collection of classic and contemporary home-baking recipes

TED SMART

This edition produced for The Book People Ltd, Hall Wood Avenue, Haydock, St Helens WA11 9UL

1 3 5 7 9 10 8 6 4 2

First published by Ebury Press
Random House, 20 Vauxhall Bridge Road, London SW1V 2SA

Random House Australia (Pty) Limited
20 Alfred Street, Milsons Point, Sydney, New South Wales 2061, Australia

Random House New Zealand Limited
18 Poland Road, Glenfield, Auckland 10, New Zealand

Random House South Africa (Pty) Limited
Endulini, 5A Jubilee Road, Parktown 2193, South Africa

The Random House Group Limited Reg. No. 954009

www.randomhouse.co.uk

A CIP catalogue record for this book is available from the British Library.

Editor: Nicky Thompson
Designers: Christine and Paul Wood

Papers used by Ebury Press are natural, recyclable products made from wood grown in sustainable forests.

Colour separation in Milan by Colorlito
Printed and bound in Spain by Graficas Estella

COOKERY NOTES

● Both metric and imperial measures are given for the recipes. Follow either set of measures, but not a mixture of both as they are not interchangeable.

● All spoon measures are level unless otherwise stated. Sets of measuring spoons are available in metric and imperial for accurate measurement of small quantities.

● Ovens should be preheated to the specified temperature. The cooking times given in the recipes assume that this has been done.

● Use large eggs except where otherwise specified. Free-range eggs are recommended.

● Where the cake should be frozen at the end of a certain stage of the method (rather than at the end), this stage is indicated.

● Preparation times and calorie counts are not given for novelty cakes as these will vary according to the expertise of the baker and the amount of icing in each slice.

CONTENTS

INTRODUCTION

There is nothing quite like the warm, enticing aroma of a freshly baked cake – and this varied collection contains recipes that will suit all kinds of occasions. Successful baking depends on the use of good basic techniques, equipment and ingredients. The following advice applies to most of the recipes.

BASIC INGREDIENTS

As with any type of cooking, the use of good basic ingredients is important. Unsalted butter gives best results in most recipes. Those who are more health-conscious may prefer to substitute margarine, but low-fat 'spreads' should be avoided as they are high in water and have a synthetic flavour. Most cake recipes require the fat to be used at room temperature. If necessary, you can soften it (cautiously) in the microwave. Eggs should also be used at room temperature to avoid curdling.

Self-raising white flour is used in most cake recipes as it has a rising agent. Plain or self-raising wholemeal flour can be substituted although the results will be darker, denser and nuttier in flavour. Half white and half wholemeal makes a good compromise, if you want to incorporate extra fibre.

Caster sugar is generally used for cakes, but light or dark muscovado sugars can be substituted for a richer colour and flavour. Other storecupboard ingredients such as nuts, dried fruits and spices are frequently included in cake recipes. Although they generally keep well, it is best not to buy them in bulk as they do eventually go stale. Keep an eye on the use-by dates.

EQUIPMENT

Little is needed in the way of special cake-making equipment for these recipes, other than accurate scales, basic bowls, spoons and so on. A hand-held electric whisk takes all the effort out of creaming and whisking, while a food processor is perfect for cakes that involve rubbing fat into the flour. To decorate some of the cakes, you will also need a piping bag and nozzles. Good-quality cake tins are essential, and

it is important to use the size stated in the recipe. Quality baking sheets are a worthwhile investment.

BAKING ADVICE

When baking cakes, always preheat the oven as required. Remember that if you have a fan oven, the temperature should be about 10°C lower than specified. Apart from very light sponges, all cakes are best left to stand in their tin for several minutes after baking to firm up slightly, before transferring to a wire rack to cool.

STORAGE

Some of the cake recipes specify storage times. With the exception of rich fruit cakes, most cakes are best enjoyed freshly baked. If storing is necessary, use a cake tin or large plastic container. Failing this, wrap the cake in greaseproof paper, then in a layer of kitchen foil. Most cakes, particularly sponges, freeze beautifully, but preferably before they are filled and decorated. If you want to freeze a gâteau, open freeze, then pack in a rigid container.

PREPARING TINS

With most cakes it is necessary to line the tins with greaseproof paper or non-stick baking parchment (which is good for roulades and meringues).

LINING A SQUARE TIN

Cut a square of greaseproof paper fractionally smaller than the base of the tin. For the sides, cut strips about 2cm (¾ inch) wider than the depth of the tin. Fold up the bottom edge by 1cm (½ inch). Grease the tin. Make a cut from the edge of the paper to the fold and press into one corner. Continue fitting the paper around the tin, cutting to fit at each corner. Lay the square of paper in the base, then grease the paper.

LINING A ROUND TIN

Place the tin on a piece of greaseproof paper and draw around it. Cut out, just inside the line. Cut strip(s) of paper, about 2cm (¾ inch) wider than the depth of the tin. Fold up the bottom edge by 1cm (½ inch), then make cuts, 2.5cm (1 inch) apart, from edge to fold. Grease tin. Position paper strip(s) around the side of the tin so the snipped edge sits on the base. Lay the paper circle in the base, then grease.

LINING A LOAF TIN
Grease the base and sides of the loaf tin. Cut a strip of greaseproof paper, the length of the tin base and wide enough to cover the base and long sides. Press into position. Cut another strip, the width of the tin base and long enough to cover the base and ends of the tin. Press into position. Grease the paper.

LINING A SHALLOW BAKING TIN
Grease the base and sides of the tin. Cut a rectangle of greaseproof or non-stick baking parchment 7.5cm (3 inches) wider and longer than the size of the tin. Press the paper into the tin, cutting the paper at the corners and folding to fit neatly. Grease the paper.

PREPARING A SANDWICH TIN
Place the sandwich tin on a piece of greaseproof paper and draw around it. Cut out, just inside the line. Grease the base and sides of the tin and fit the paper into the base. Grease the paper. Sprinkle a little flour into the tin. Tap and tilt the tin until flour coats the base and sides. Tip out any excess flour.

PROTECTING A FRUIT CAKE
To prevent the edges of a fruit cake overcooking, wrap the tin in brown paper. First, line the inside, then cut a double thick strip of brown paper the circumference of the tin and 2.5cm (1 inch) deeper. Position around the tin, securing with string.

CAKE-MAKING TECHNIQUES
To use the creaming method, beat together the softened butter or margarine and sugar until pale and fluffy and very light in consistency. Use an electric whisk or a wooden spoon (which will take longer). Then beat in the eggs, a little at a time, beating well after each addition. Sift the flour over the creamed mixture, sifting high to incorporate plenty of air. Use a large metal spoon to gently fold in the flour, cutting and folding into the mixture using a figure-of-eight movement. Spoon the cake mixture into the tin, dividing it equally if making a sandwich cake. Use a palette knife to spread the mixture evenly, right to the edges.

To use the whisking method, put the eggs and sugar in a large heatproof bowl over a pan of hot water and whisk until the mixture is thick enough to leave a trail when the whisk is lifted from the bowl. Remove the bowl from the heat and continue whisking for about 5 minutes or until cool. Sift the flour over the mixture. Using a large metal spoon, gently cut and fold the flour into the whisked mixture. Sift the remaining flour onto the mixture and lightly fold in. Do not overmix or the sponge will reduce in volume. Pour the whisked mixture into the tin and tilt the tin so that the mixture spreads to the edges. If necessary, use a spatula to spread the mixture gently into the corners. Avoid over-spreading as this will crush the air bubbles.

TESTING CAKES AFTER BAKING
To test a sponge, carefully remove the cake from the oven and touch the cake with one hand. It should feel spongy and give very lightly. With whisked cakes, the sponge should just be shrinking from the sides of the tin. If necessary, return the cake to the oven for a few minutes, closing the door gently so that the vibration does not cause the cake to sink in the middle.

To test a fruit cake, remove the cake from the oven, insert a skewer into the centre and remove. The skewer should come away cleanly. If any cake mixture is sticking to the skewer, return the cake to the oven for a little longer.

TURNING OUT CAKES
Remove sponge cakes from the tin immediately after baking. Loosen the edges and then invert onto a wire cooling rack. If preferred, place a sheet of non-stick baking parchment dusted with sugar over the rack before inverting, so that the sponge does not stick to the rack. Leave semi-rich fruit cakes to cool in the tin for about 15 minutes. Rich fruit cakes should be left to cool completely in the tin as they tend to break up if removed while still warm.

BEST CLASSIC RECIPES

TRADITIONAL MADEIRA CAKE

This is a good moist plain cake which has a firm texture, making it a good base for a celebration or novelty cake. There are many variations for flavouring. Refer to the cake chart (opposite) for sizes and quantities. The smallest cake will produce about 12 slices (245 cals per slice).

1 Grease and line a deep cake tin.

2 Sift the flours together. Cream the butter and sugar in a bowl until pale and fluffy. Add the eggs, a little at a time, beating well after each addition.

3 Fold in the flour with a plastic spatula, adding a little lemon juice or milk if necessary to give a dropping consistency. Add any flavourings, if required.

4 Turn the mixture into the prepared tin and spread it out evenly. Give the tin a sharp tap to remove any air pockets. Make a depression in the centre of the mixture to ensure a level surface.

5 Bake in the centre of the oven at 170°C/325°F/gas 3 following the chart baking times. When cooked, the surface of the cake should be a deep golden colour and should feel firm to the touch.

6 Leave the cake to cool in the tin, then remove and cool completely on a wire rack. Wrap in cling film or foil and store in a cool place until required.

QUICK-MIX MADEIRA CAKE

1 Grease and line a deep cake tin.

2 Sift the flours into a mixing bowl, add the butter or margarine, sugar, eggs and lemon juice or milk. Mix with a wooden spoon, then beat for 1–2 minutes until smooth and glossy. Alternatively, use an electric mixer and beat for 1 minute only. Add any flavourings, if required, and beat until well blended.

3 Turn the mixture into the prepared tin and spread it out evenly. Give the tin a sharp tap to remove any air pockets. Make a depression in the centre of the mixture to ensure a level surface.

4 Bake as for the traditional method (see stage 5).

VARIATIONS
These flavourings are for a 3-egg quantity of Madeira cake. Increase the suggested flavourings to suit the quantities being made.
Cherry cake: Add 175g (6oz) glacé cherries, halved.
Coconut cake: Add 50g (2oz) desiccated coconut.
Nutty cake: Replace 125g (4oz) flour with ground almonds, hazelnuts, walnuts or pecan nuts.
Citrus cake: Add the grated rind and juice of 1 lemon, orange or lime.

MADEIRA CAKE CHART

CAKE TIN SIZE	15cm (6 inch) square 18cm (7 inch) round	18cm (7 inch) square 20cm (8 inch) round	20cm (8 inch) square 23cm (9 inch) round	23cm (9 inch) square 25cm (10 inch) round
Plain flour	125g (4oz)	175g (6oz)	225g (8oz)	250g (9oz)
Self-raising flour	125g (4oz)	175g (6oz)	225g (8oz)	250g (9oz)
Butter or margarine	175g (6oz)	275g (10oz)	400g (14oz)	450g (1lb)
Caster sugar	175g (6oz)	275g (10oz)	400g (14oz)	450g (1lb)
Eggs	3	5	7	8
Lemon juice or milk	30ml (2 tbsp)	45ml (3 tbsp)	52.5ml (3½ tbsp)	60ml (4 tbsp)
Baking time (approx.)	1¼–1½ hours	1½–1¾ hours	1¾–2 hours	1¾–2 hours

CAKE TIN SIZE	25cm (10 inch) square 28cm (11 inch) round	28cm (11 inch) square 30cm (12 inch) round	30cm (12 inch) square 33cm (13 inch) round
Plain flour	275g (10oz)	350g (12oz)	450g (1lb)
Self-raising flour	275g (10oz)	350g (12oz)	450g (1lb)
Butter or margarine	500g (1lb 2oz)	625g (1lb 6oz)	725g (1lb 10oz)
Caster sugar	500g (1lb 2oz)	625g (1lb 6oz)	725g (1lb 10oz)
Eggs	10	12	13
Lemon juice or milk	67.5ml (4½ tbsp)	75ml (5 tbsp)	82.5ml (5½ tbsp)
Baking time (approx.)	2–2¼ hours	2¼–2½ hours	2½–2¾ hours

TOP TIPS

• To ensure the cake mixture does not curdle, always use eggs at room temperature and beat thoroughly after adding each egg. If it curdles, a heavier cake will result. To prevent curdling, add a little of the measured flour with the eggs.

• For best results, bake with unsalted butter. Make sure the butter or margarine is softened before use.

TRADITIONAL VICTORIA SANDWICH CAKE

This popular English cake produces a light sponge which may be flavoured and cooked in different shapes and sizes of tins.

Makes 8 slices
Preparation: 25 minutes, plus cooling
Cooking time: 25–30 minutes
Freezing: suitable
370 cals per slice

175g (6oz) butter or block margarine, softened

175g (6oz) caster sugar

3 eggs, beaten

175g (6oz) self-raising flour, sifted

1 Grease and base-line two 18cm (7 inch) sandwich tins with greaseproof paper or non-stick baking parchment. Grease the paper.

2 Beat the butter or margarine and sugar together until pale and fluffy. Add the eggs, a little at a time, beating well.

3 Fold in half the flour, using a spatula, then fold in the remainder until it is incorporated.

4 Divide the mixture evenly between the tins and level with a palette knife. Bake in the centre of the oven at 180°C/350°F/gas 4 for 25–30 minutes until the cakes are well risen and spring back when lightly pressed in the centre. Loosen the edges of the cakes with a palette knife and leave in the tins for 5 minutes. Turn out, invert onto a wire rack, remove the lining paper and leave to cool.

QUICK-MIX VICTORIA SPONGE

Makes 8 slices
Preparation: 25 minutes, plus cooling
Cooking time: 25–30 minutes
Freezing: suitable
370 cals per slice

175g (6oz) self-raising flour, sifted

5ml (1 tsp) baking powder

175g (6oz) caster sugar

175g (6oz) soft margarine

3 eggs, beaten

1 Grease and base-line two 18cm (7 inch) sandwich tins with greaseproof paper or non-stick baking parchment. Grease the paper.

2 Sift the flour and baking powder into a bowl. Add the sugar, margarine and eggs. Mix with a wooden spoon, beat for 1–2 minutes until smooth and glossy, or use an electric mixer or food processor.

3 Bake as for the traditional method (see stage 4).

VARIATIONS
Chocolate sandwich cake: Replace 45ml (3 tbsp) flour with sifted cocoa powder.
Coffee sandwich cake: Blend together 10ml (2 tsp) instant coffee granules with 15ml (1 tbsp) boiling water. Cool and add to the mixture with the eggs.
Citrus sandwich cake: Add the finely grated rind of 1 orange, lime or lemon to the mixture.

TOP TIP
Check that the fat is softened before mixing with the remaining ingredients. If the mixture seems firm once creamed, beat in a dash of milk so that it drops easily from the spoon when gently tapped against the bowl.

RICH FRUIT CAKE

This recipe makes a very moist rich cake suitable for any celebration cake. It can be made in stages, which is convenient if time is short or if you are making more than one cake. Most dried fruit is sold ready cleaned and dried so it does not need to be washed before use. The fruit can be weighed and mixed a day ahead, the tins prepared and lined in advance, and other ingredients weighed ready to mix. On the day of baking simply make the cake and bake.

The quantities have been carefully worked out so that the depth of each cake is the same. This is important when making several tiers for a wedding cake as they must all be the same depth to look aesthetically correct. For sizes and quantities, refer to the chart (overleaf). Use the same amount of brandy stated for the cake to 'feed' the cake after baking. Spoon half the amount over the surface after baking and the remainder about a week later.

1 Grease and line the appropriate cake tin for the size of cake you wish to make, using a double thickness of greaseproof paper. Tie a double band of brown paper round the outside (see Protecting a Fruit Cake on page 9). Stand the tin on a baking sheet, double lined with brown paper.

2 Prepare the ingredients for the appropriate size of cake according to the chart (overleaf). Place the currants, sultanas, raisins, glacé cherries, mixed peel and flaked almonds in a large mixing bowl. Mix all the ingredients together until well blended, then cover the bowl with cling film. Leave for several hours or overnight in a cool place if required.

3 Sift the flour, mixed spice and cinnamon together into another mixing bowl.

4 Put the butter, sugar and grated lemon rind into a bowl and cream together until pale and fluffy. Add the beaten eggs gradually, beating well after each addition.

5 Gradually fold the flour lightly into the mixture with a plastic-bladed spatula, then fold in the brandy. Finally fold in the fruit and the nuts until evenly distributed throughout the mixture.

6 Spoon the mixture into the prepared tin and spread evenly. Give the tin a few sharp taps to level the mixture and to remove any air pockets. Smooth the surface with the back of a metal spoon, making a slight depression in the centre.

7 Bake in the centre of the oven at 150°C/300°F/ gas 2, using the time suggested in the chart as an approximate guide. If the cake is not cooked, return to the oven, re-testing at 15-minute intervals. Remove the cake from the oven and allow it to cool in the tin.

8 Turn the cake out of the tin but do not remove the lining paper as it helps to keep the cake moist. Prick the top all over with a fine skewer and spoon over half the quantity of brandy listed in the recipe. Wrap in a double thickness of foil.

9 Store the cake, the right way up, in a cool dry place for 1 week. Unwrap and spoon over the remaining brandy. Re-wrap and store the cake upside down, so the brandy moistens the top of the cake and helps to keep it flat. The cake will keep well for up to 2–3 months. For longer storage, freeze the cake, making sure that it is completely thawed before applying the almond paste and icing.

TOP TIP
When baking large cakes (25cm/10 inch and upwards), it is advisable to reduce the oven heat to 130°C/250°F/ gas 1 after two-thirds of the baking time.

RICH FRUIT CAKE CHART

CAKE TIN	12cm (5 inch) square 15cm (6 inch) round	15cm (6 inch) square 18cm (7 inch) round	18cm (7 inch) square 20cm (8 inch) round	20cm (8 inch) square 23cm (9 inch) round
Currants	225g (8oz)	350g (12oz)	450g (1lb)	625g (1lb 6oz)
Sultanas	100g (4oz)	125g (4½oz)	200g (7oz)	225g (8oz)
Raisins	100g (4oz)	125g (4½oz)	200g (7oz)	225g (8oz)
Glacé cherries	50g (2oz)	75g (3oz)	150g (5oz)	175g (6oz)
Mixed peel	25g (1oz)	50g (2oz)	75g (3oz)	100g (4oz)
Flaked almonds	25g (1oz)	50g (2oz)	75g (3oz)	100g (4oz)
Lemon rind	a little	a little	a little	¼ lemon
Plain flour	175g (6oz)	215g (7½oz)	350g (12oz)	400g (14oz)
Mixed spice	1.25ml (¼ tsp)	2.5ml (½ tsp)	2.5ml (½ tsp)	5ml (1 tsp)
Cinnamon	1.25ml (¼ tsp)	2.5ml (½ tsp)	2.5ml (½ tsp)	5ml (1 tsp)
Butter	150g (5oz)	175g (6oz)	275g (10oz)	350g (12oz)
Soft brown sugar	150g (5oz)	175g (6oz)	275g (10oz)	350g (12oz)
Eggs, beaten	2½	3	5	6
Brandy	15ml (1 tbsp)	15ml (1 tbsp)	15–30ml (1–2 tbsp)	30ml (2 tbsp)
Baking time	2½–3 hours	3½ hours	3½ hours	4 hours
Cooked weight	1.1kg (2½lb)	1.5kg (3¼lb)	2.1kg (4¾lb)	2.7kg (6lb)

CAKE TIN	23cm (9 inch) square 25cm (10 inch) round	25cm (10 inch) square 28cm (11 inch) round	28cm (11 inch) square 30cm (12 inch) round	30cm (11 inch) square 33cm (12 inch) round
Currants	775g (1lb 12oz)	1.1kg (2lb 8oz)	1.5kg (3lb 2oz)	1.7kg (3lb 12oz)
Sultanas	375g (13oz)	400g (14oz)	525g (1lb 3oz)	625g (1lb 6oz)
Raisins	375g (13oz)	400g (14oz)	525g (1lb 3oz)	625g (1lb 6oz)
Glacé cherries	250g (9oz)	275g (10oz)	350g (12oz)	425g (15oz)
Mixed peel	150g (5oz)	200g (7oz)	250g (9oz)	275g (10oz)
Flaked almonds	150g (5oz)	200g (7oz)	250g (9oz)	275g (10oz)
Lemon rind	¼ lemon	½ lemon	½ lemon	1 lemon
Plain flour	600g (1lb 5oz)	700g (1lb 8oz)	825g (1lb 13oz)	1kg (2lb 6oz)
Mixed spice	5ml (1 tsp)	10ml (2 tsp)	12.5ml (2½ tsp)	12.5ml (2½ tsp)
Cinnamon	5ml (1 tsp)	10ml (2 tsp)	12.5ml (2½ tsp)	12.5ml (2½ tsp)
Butter	500g (1lb 2oz)	600g (1lb 5oz)	800g (1lb 12oz)	950g (2lb 2oz)
Soft brown sugar	500g (1lb 2oz)	600g (1lb 5oz)	800g (1lb 12oz)	950g (2lb 2oz)
Eggs, beaten	9	11	14	17
Brandy	30–45ml (2–3 tbsp)	45ml (3 tbsp)	60ml (4 tbsp)	90ml (6 tbsp)
Baking time	4½ hours	6 hours	6–6½ hours	6½ hours
Cooked weight	3.8kg (8½lb)	4.8kg (10¾lb)	6.1kg (13½lb)	7.4kg (16½lb)

APRICOT GLAZE

Makes 150ml (¼ pint)
Preparation: 5 minutes
Cooking time: 2 minutes
Freezing: suitable
55 cals per 25ml (1fl oz)

125g (4oz) apricot jam
30ml (2 tbsp) water

1 Place the jam and the water in a small pan. Heat gently, stirring, until the jam begins to melt. Bring to the boil and simmer for 1 minute.

2 Strain the jam through a nylon sieve. Use while still warm.

ALMOND PASTE

Makes 450g (1lb)
Preparation: 10 minutes
Freezing: suitable
135 cals per 25g (1oz)

225g (8oz) ground almonds
125g (4oz) caster sugar
125g (4oz) icing sugar
1 egg
5ml (1 tsp) lemon juice
5ml (1 tsp) sherry
1–2 drops of vanilla essence

1 Place the ground almonds, caster sugar and icing sugar in a bowl and mix together. In a separate bowl, whisk the egg with the remaining ingredients and add to the dry mixture.

2 Stir well to mix, pounding gently to release some of the oil from the almonds. Knead with your hands until smooth. Cover until ready to use.

TOP TIP
If you prefer not to use raw egg to bind the paste, mix the other liquid ingredients with a little water instead.

COVERING A CAKE WITH ALMOND PASTE

Almond paste or marzipan is applied to rich fruit cakes to create a smooth foundation for the icing. It is therefore important to apply it neatly. You can either make your own paste (see page 17) or buy it. Choose white, rather than yellow, almond paste, as it is less likely to discolour the icing. Home-made almond paste inevitably has a superior flavour. Allow time for the almond paste to dry before covering with icing. Home-made icing takes longer to dry out than ready-made. Refer to the chart on page 20 for quantities.

1 Trim the top of the cake level. Turn the cake over so that the flat bottom becomes the top.

2 Roll out half the almond paste on a surface dusted with icing sugar to fit the top of the cake. Brush the top of the cake with apricot glaze (see page 17).

3 Lift the almond paste on top of the cake and smooth over, neatening the edges. Place on a cake board, which should be at least 5cm (2 inches) larger than the cake.

4 Cut a piece of string the same height as the cake with its almond paste top, and another to fit round the side of the cake. Roll out the remaining almond paste and, using the string as a guide, trim the paste to size. Brush the sides of the cake and the almond paste rim with apricot glaze.

5 Roll up the almond paste strip loosely. Place one end against the side of the cake and unroll to cover it. Use a palette knife to smooth over the sides and joins of the paste.

6 Flatten the top lightly with a rolling pin. Leave the cake to dry in a cool, dry place to dry out thoroughly for at least 2 days before applying smooth royal icing. Ready-to-roll icing can be applied after 24 hours.

BUTTER CREAM

75g (3oz) unsalted butter, softened
175g (6oz) icing sugar, sifted
a few drops of vanilla essence
15–30ml (1–2 tbsp) milk or water

1 Put the butter in a bowl and beat with a wooden spoon until it is light and fluffy.

2 Gradually stir in the icing sugar, vanilla and milk or water. Beat well until light and smooth.

VARIATIONS

Orange, lime or lemon: Replace the vanilla essence with a little finely grated orange, lime or lemon rind. Add a little juice from the fruit instead of the milk, beating well to avoid curdling the mixture. If the icing is to be piped, omit the fruit rind.

Coffee: Replace the vanilla essence with 10ml (2 tsp) instant coffee granules dissolved in 15ml (1 tbsp) boiling water; cool before adding to the mixture.

Chocolate: Blend 15ml (1 tbsp) cocoa powder with 30ml (2 tbsp) boiling water and cool before adding to the mixture.

ROYAL ICING

Refer to the chart (below) for the amount of icing needed to cover different cake sizes and shapes. Note that it is better not to make up more than 900g (2lb) of icing at a time as smaller amounts keep better. The quantities in the chart will give you enough icing for 2–3 coats (depending on how skilful you are).

Makes 450g (1lb)
Preparation: 20 minutes
100 cals per 25g (1oz)

2 egg whites or 15ml (1 tbsp) albumen powder
10ml (2 tsp) liquid glycerine (optional, see Top Tip)
450g (1lb) icing sugar

1 If using the egg whites and the glycerine, place them in a bowl and stir just enough to break up the egg whites. If using albumen powder, mix according to the manufacturer's instructions.

2 Using a clean wooden spoon, add a little sieved icing sugar and start mixing gently, to incorporate as little air as possible.

3 Add a little more icing sugar as the mixture becomes lighter. Continue to add the sugar, stirring gently but thoroughly until the mixture is stiff and stands in soft peaks. If required for coating, it should form soft peaks; for piping it should be a little stiffer.

4 Transfer to an airtight container, cover the icing closely with cling film to exclude air and prevent the surface of the icing drying out, and then seal. When required, stir the icing slowly.

> TOP TIP
> Glycerine keeps the icing from becoming hard. Omit the glycerine if the icing is to cover a tiered cake, as a very hard surface is needed to support the tiers.

QUANTITY GUIDE FOR ALMOND PASTE, READY-TO-ROLL ICING (SUGAR PASTE) AND ROYAL ICING

SQUARE TIN	ROUND TIN	ALMOND PASTE	READY-TO-ROLL ICING	ROYAL ICING
12cm (5 inch)	15cm (6 inch)	350g (12oz)	350g (12oz)	450g (1lb)
15cm (6 inch)	18cm (7 inch)	450g (1lb)	450g (1lb)	550g (1¼lb)
18cm (7 inch)	20cm (8 inch)	550g (1¼lb)	700g (1½lb)	700g (1½lb)
20cm (8 inch)	23cm (9 inch)	800g (1¾lb)	800g (1¾lb)	900g (2lb)
23cm (9 inch)	25cm (10 inch)	900g (2lb)	900g (2lb)	1kg (2¼lb)
25cm (10 inch)	28cm (11 inch)	1kg (2¼lb)	1kg (2¼lb)	1.1kg (2½lb)
28cm (11 inch)	30cm (12 inch)	1.1kg (2½lb)	1.1kg (2½lb)	1.4kg (3lb)
30cm (12 inch)	33cm (13 inch)	1.4kg (3lb)	1.4kg (3lb)	1.6kg (3½lb)
33cm (13 inch)	35cm (14 inch)	1.6kg (3½lb)	1.6kg (3½lb)	1.8kg (4lb)

APPLYING FLAT ROYAL ICING

1 Always apply royal icing over a layer of almond paste (see pages 18–19). Put a large spoonful of icing onto the centre of the cake and spread it out, using a palette knife in a paddling motion.

2 Draw an icing ruler across the top of the cake towards you, applying an even pressure and keeping the ruler at an angle of about 30°. Remove surplus icing by running a palette knife around the edge, at right angles to the cake.

3 To cover the sides, for best results, place a round cake on a turntable. Spread icing onto the sides using the same paddling motion. Hold a cake scraper at an angle of 45° and draw it around the side, then pull it off quickly to leave only a slight mark. Leave to dry in a cool place for 24 hours. Keep the remaining icing well covered and sealed.

4 The next day, scrape away any rough icing from the top edge with a small sharp knife (or use clean fine sandpaper). Brush off loose icing with a clean pastry brush. Apply 2 or 3 further coats, allowing each to dry overnight before applying the next. Leave to dry overnight before applying any decorations.

APPLYING READY-TO-ROLL ICING (SUGAR PASTE)

1 Dust the work surface and rolling pin with cornflour. Knead the icing until pliable. Roll out into a round or square 5–7.5cm (2–3 inches) larger than the cake all round.

2 With the help of a rolling pin, lift the icing on top of the cake and allow it to drape over the edges. Dust your hands with cornflour and press the icing onto the sides of the cake, easing it down to the board.

3 Trim off the excess icing at the base to neaten.

4 Using your fingers dusted with a little cornflour, gently rub the surface in a circular movement to buff the icing and make it smooth.

CARROT CAKE

Makes 8–10 slices
Preparation: 25 minutes, plus cooling
Cooking time: 35–40 minutes
Freezing: suitable (stage 3)
735–570 cals per slice

350g (12oz) carrots
125g (4oz) brazil nuts
225g (8oz) unsalted butter or margarine, softened
225g (8oz) caster sugar
175g (6oz) self-raising white flour
5ml (1 tsp) baking powder
2.5ml (½ tsp) ground allspice
4 eggs
grated rind of 1 orange
15ml (1 tbsp) orange juice
50g (2oz) ground almonds

FROSTING
250g (9oz) mascarpone or low-fat cream cheese
5ml (1 tsp) finely grated orange rind (optional)
30ml (2 tbsp) orange juice
30ml (2 tbsp) icing sugar

TO DECORATE
1 large carrot
oil, for frying
icing sugar, for dusting

1 Preheat the oven to 180°C/350°F/gas 4. Grease and base-line two 18cm (7 inch) sandwich tins. Dust the sides of the tins with flour and shake out the excess. Peel and finely grate the carrots. Coarsely chop the brazil nuts and lightly toast them.

2 Cream the butter or margarine and sugar together in a bowl until pale and fluffy. Sift the flour, baking powder and allspice into the bowl. Add the eggs, orange rind and juice, and the ground almonds; beat well. Stir in the carrots and brazil nuts.

3 Divide the mixture between the tins and level the surfaces. Bake for 35–40 minutes until risen and firm to touch. Transfer to a wire rack to cool.

4 For the topping, beat the cheese, orange rind if using, orange juice and icing sugar together in a bowl until smooth. Use half to sandwich the cakes together. Spread the remainder over the top of the cake, swirling it attractively.

5 For the decoration, peel the carrot and pare into long thin ribbons, using a swivel vegetable peeler. Dry the carrot ribbons on kitchen paper. Heat a 1cm (½ inch) depth of oil in a frying pan until a piece of carrot added to the hot oil sizzles on the surface. Fry the carrots, in two batches, until they shrink and turn golden. Drain with a slotted spoon and dry on kitchen paper.

6 Scatter the carrot pieces over the top of the cake and dust with icing sugar. Chill until ready to serve.

TOP TIP
It is important to dry the carrot ribbons thoroughly before frying to ensure a crisp result.

STICKY GINGERBREAD

Makes 12 slices
Preparation: 20 minutes
Cooking time: 1 hour 20 minutes
Freezing: suitable
350 cals per slice

150g (5oz) preserved stem ginger in syrup, plus
45ml (3 tbsp) syrup from jar

1 large cooking apple, about 225g (8oz)

15ml (1 tbsp) lemon juice

125g (4oz) black treacle

125g (4oz) golden syrup

175g (6oz) molasses or dark muscovado sugar

175g (6oz) unsalted butter

225g (8oz) plain white flour

125g (4oz) plain wholemeal flour

5ml (1 tsp) ground mixed spice

7.5ml (1½ tsp) bicarbonate of soda

2 eggs

1 Preheat the oven to 160°C/325°F/gas 3. Grease and line a deep 18cm (7 inch) square cake tin. Thinly slice the ginger pieces. Peel, core and quarter the apple; immerse in a bowl of water with the lemon juice added to prevent discoloration.

2 Put the treacle, syrup and sugar in a saucepan. Cut the butter into pieces and add to the pan. Heat gently until the butter melts; leave to cool slightly.

3 Sift the flours, spice and bicarbonate of soda into a bowl. Grate three-quarters of the apple into the bowl and toss lightly in the flour. Add the melted mixture, eggs and three-quarters of the ginger pieces. Beat well until thoroughly combined.

4 Turn the mixture into the prepared tin, spreading it into the corners. Using a potato peeler, pare the remaining apple into thin slices. Scatter the apple slices and remaining ginger over the surface of the gingerbread and press down lightly into the mixture with the tip of a knife. Bake for 1 hour 20 minutes or until firm to the touch. Leave to cool in the tin.

TOP TIP
Gingerbread will keep well in an airtight tin for up to 1 week. It's best stored for several days before eating.

VARIATION
For a 'hotter' flavour add 10ml (2 tsp) ground ginger with the mixed spice.

PANETTONE

Makes 10–12 slices
Preparation: 25 minutes, plus rising
Cooking time: 35 minutes
Freezing: suitable
415–320 cals per slice

450g (1lb) strong plain white flour

10ml (2 tsp) salt

75g (3oz) caster sugar

1½ x 7g (¼oz) sachets fast-action dried yeast

finely grated rind of 1 lemon

finely grated rind of 1 orange

1 egg

4 egg yolks

150ml (¼ pint) warm milk

175g (6oz) unsalted butter, softened

75g (3oz) chopped mixed candied orange and citron peel

125g (4oz) raisins

1 Line a 15cm (6 inch) deep cake tin with a double layer of non-stick baking parchment which extends 12cm (5 inches) above the rim.

2 Sift the flour and salt into a bowl and stir in the sugar, yeast and citrus rinds. Make a well in the centre. Beat the egg and egg yolks together and add to the well with the warm milk. Mix to an elastic dough, adding a little more flour if necessary, but keeping the dough quite soft. Work in the softened butter.

3 Cover with cling film and leave to rise for 2–4 hours until doubled in volume.

4 Knock back the dough and knead in the chopped peel and raisins. Place in the prepared tin and cut a deep cross on the top with a very sharp knife. Cover and leave to rise until the dough is 2.5cm (1 inch) above the top of the tin.

5 Bake at 200°C/400°F/gas 6 for 15 minutes, then lower the heat to 180°C/350°F/gas 4 and bake for a further 40 minutes until well risen and golden. Leave in the tin for 10 minutes, then transfer to a wire rack to cool.

6 To serve, cut off the top and slice horizontally. To store, replace the top, wrap the whole panettone in cling film or foil and refrigerate. Bring to room temperature to serve.

TOP TIP
Most sweet egg and butter enriched doughs take a long time to rise, so start them early in the day. Don't put them to rise in a very warm place once the butter is incorporated, or it will melt and make the dough greasy.

STOLLEN

Makes 10 slices
Preparation: 20 minutes, plus rising
Cooking time: 40 minutes
Freezing: not suitable
320 cals per slice

350g (12oz) strong plain white flour

2.5ml (½ tsp) salt

2.5ml (½ tsp) ground mixed spice

50g (2oz) unsalted butter, diced

7g (¼oz) sachet fast-action dried yeast

25g (1oz) caster sugar

125g (4oz) mixed sultanas, currants and raisins

25g (1oz) glacé cherries or ready-to-eat dried apricots, chopped

25g (1oz) chopped mixed peel

50g (2oz) chopped almonds

1 small egg, beaten

120–150ml (4–5ml) warmed milk

125g (4oz) ready-made almond paste

icing sugar, for dusting

1 Sift the flour, salt and spice into a bowl and rub in the butter. Stir in the rest of the ingredients, except the almond paste, adding sufficient warm milk to mix to a soft dough.

2 Turn onto a lightly floured surface and knead for about 10 minutes, then shape into a ball. Place in an oiled bowl, cover and leave to rise in a warm place for 2 hours or until doubled in size.

3 Knock back the dough, then shape into a long oval about 1cm (½ inch) deep.

4 Roll the almond paste into a log, a little shorter than the length of the oval. Make a slight indentation along the length of the dough. Lay the almond paste in this groove and fold the dough over to enclose it. Press the edges together to seal.

5 Transfer to a lightly oiled large baking sheet, cover and leave to rise for a further 30 minutes.

6 Bake at 180°C/350°F/gas 4 for 40 minutes. Transfer to a wire rack to cool. Serve dusted with icing sugar. Eat within 1–2 days.

VANILLA KUGELHOPF

Makes 10 slices
Preparation: 15 minutes, plus rising
Cooking time: 25–30 minutes
Freezing: suitable
295 cals per slice

125g (4oz) unsalted butter

250g (9oz) plain white flour

pinch of salt

10ml (2 tsp) fast-action dried yeast

40g (1½oz) caster sugar

15g (½oz) vanilla sugar (or caster sugar and a generous splash of vanilla essence)

grated rind of 1 lemon

50g (2oz) chopped mixed peel

25g (1oz) glacé cherries, finely chopped

45ml (3 tbsp) milk

3 eggs

icing sugar, for dusting

SPICED BUTTER
75g (3oz) unsalted butter, softened

15ml (1 tbsp) icing sugar

1.25ml (¼ tsp) ground nutmeg

2.5ml (½ tsp) ground mixed spice

1.25ml (¼ tsp) ground ginger

1 Melt the butter and leave to cool slightly. Sift the flour and salt into a bowl. Add the yeast, sugars, lemon rind, chopped peel and cherries.

2 Beat the melted butter with the milk and eggs. Add to the bowl and beat well for 2 minutes. Cover the bowl with cling film and leave in a warm place until the mixture has doubled in size.

3 Meanwhile, make the spiced butter. Beat the ingredients together in a bowl until thoroughly combined. Turn into a small serving dish and keep in a cool place.

4 Preheat the oven to 200°C/400°F/gas 6. Brush a 20cm (8 inch) kugelhopf tin or 1.7 litre (3 pint) ring tin with a little melted white vegetable fat. Dust with flour and shake out the excess.

5 Lightly beat the risen dough to reduce the volume, then turn into the prepared tin. Cover with oiled cling film and leave to rise until the dough almost reaches the top of the tin.

6 Bake the kugelhopf for 25–30 minutes until golden. Leave in the tin for 5 minutes, then loosen the edges with a knife. Invert the tin onto a wire rack and tap the cake out. Cool slightly before serving, dusted with icing sugar and accompanied by the spiced butter.

TOP TIP
Although very easy to make, you need to allow plenty of time for the dough to rise. This might take 2 hours for the first proving and a further 1 hour in the tin.

BEST CHOCOLATE CAKES

DARK MOIST CHOCOLATE CAKE

Makes 12 slices
Preparation: 30 minutes
Cooking time: 1¼–1½ hours
Freezing: suitable (stage 5)
460 cals per slice

250g (9oz) good quality plain chocolate (70% cocoa solids), in pieces

90ml (3fl oz) milk

175g (6oz) unsalted butter, softened

175g (6oz) light muscovado sugar

4 eggs

150g (5oz) self-raising white flour

75g (3oz) ground almonds

TOPPING
100g (3½oz) good quality plain chocolate (70% cocoa solids), in pieces

25g (1oz) unsalted butter

TO DECORATE
25g (1oz) milk chocolate, melted

1 Grease and line a 20cm (8 inch) round, deep cake tin.

2 Melt the chocolate with the milk in a heatproof bowl over a pan of simmering water; stir until smooth. Let the mixture cool slightly.

3 Cream the butter and sugar together in a bowl until light and fluffy. Gradually beat in the eggs, adding a little of the flour to prevent curdling. Stir in the melted chocolate mixture.

4 Sift in the remaining flour and add the ground almonds. Fold in lightly until evenly combined.

5 Turn the mixture into the prepared tin and level the surface. Bake at 170°C/325°F/gas 3 for 1¼–1½ hours until a skewer inserted into the centre comes out clean. Leave in the tin for 5 minutes, then transfer to a wire rack to cool, placing the cake the right way up.

6 For the topping, melt the chocolate and butter in a heatproof bowl over a pan of simmering water. Stir until smooth. Let the melted chocolate cool for a few minutes until slightly thickened, then spread on top of the cake using a palette knife. Leave to set in a cool place. Drizzle with the melted milk chocolate to decorate.

CHOCOLATE GÂTEAU

Makes 16 slices
Preparation: 35 minutes, plus cooling
Cooking time: 25–30 minutes
Freezing: suitable (stage 3)
475 cals per slice

75g (3oz) bitter chocolate

175g (6oz) unsalted butter, softened

300g (10oz) light muscovado sugar

3 eggs

300g (10oz) plain white flour

5ml (1 tsp) bicarbonate of soda

10ml (2 tsp) baking powder

150ml (¼ pint) soured cream

FILLING
175g (6oz) no-need-to-soak dried prunes

5ml (1 tsp) vanilla essence

2.5ml (½ tsp) cornflour

90ml (6 tbsp) brandy

TO DECORATE
450ml (¾ pint) double cream

250ml (8fl oz) crème fraîche

cocoa powder, for dusting

1 Preheat the oven to 190°C/375°F/gas 5. Grease and base-line three 20cm (8 inch) sandwich tins. Break up the chocolate and heat very gently in a saucepan with 150ml (¼ pint) water until melted. Cool slightly.

2 Cream the butter and sugar together in a bowl until pale and fluffy. Gradually beat in the eggs, a little at a time, adding a little of the flour to prevent curdling. Sift together the remaining flour, bicarbonate of soda and baking powder.

3 Stir the chocolate into the creamed mixture, then fold in the flour and soured cream. Divide between the prepared tins and level the surfaces. Bake for 25–30 minutes until firm to the touch. Turn out and cool on a wire rack.

4 For the filling, roughly chop the prunes and place in a saucepan with 90ml (3fl oz) water, and the vanilla essence. Bring to the boil, reduce the heat and simmer gently for 5 minutes. Blend the cornflour with 15ml (1 tbsp) water, add to the pan and cook, stirring, for 1 minute until thickened. Remove from the heat and add the brandy. Leave to cool.

5 For the decoration, whip the cream until just holding its shape. Fold in the crème fraîche.

6 Spread the prune filling on two of the sponges, then cover with a little of the cream. Assemble the three layers on a serving plate and cover with the remaining cream, swirling it attractively. Serve dusted with cocoa powder.

TOP TIP
The prune filling, once cooled, should be very moist, with juices still visible. Add a little extra liqueur or water if it has become dry.

PRALINE GÂTEAU

Makes 16 slices
Preparation: 1 hour, plus cooling
Cooking time: 1¼–1½ hours
Freezing: suitable (stage 3)
545 cals per slice

250g (9oz) plain chocolate

90ml (3fl oz) amaretto liqueur

175g (6oz) unsalted butter, softened

175g (6oz) light muscovado sugar

4 eggs

150g (5oz) self-raising white flour

75g (3oz) ground almonds

FILLING
100g (3½oz) whole blanched almonds

125g (4oz) caster sugar

250ml (8fl oz) double cream

GANACHE
175g (6oz) plain chocolate

175ml (6fl oz) double cream

1 Preheat the oven to 160°C/325°F/gas 3. Grease and line a 20cm (8 inch) round cake tin. Break the chocolate into a heatproof bowl, add the liqueur and leave until melted; stir until smooth.

2 Cream the butter and sugar together in a bowl until pale and fluffy. Gradually beat in the eggs, adding a little of the flour to prevent curdling. Stir in the melted chocolate. Sift the remaining flour into the bowl and sprinkle in the ground almonds. Lightly fold into the mixture.

3 Turn into the prepared tin and level the surface. Bake for 1¼–1½ hours until well risen and a skewer, inserted into the centre, comes out clean. Cool in the tin.

4 For the filling, toast the nuts until evenly golden. Put the sugar in a heavy-based pan with 50ml (2fl oz) water. Heat gently until dissolved, then stir in the nuts. Bring to the boil and boil until the syrup begins to brown. Pour onto a lightly oiled baking sheet, leave to cool and harden, then crush finely.

5 Lightly whip the cream and stir in all but 45ml (3 tbsp) praline. Split the cake into three layers. Re-assemble, sandwiching the layers with the praline cream.

6 For the ganache, break the chocolate into pieces. Bring the cream to the boil in a heavy-based saucepan. Add the chocolate, remove from the heat and stir until smooth. Leave to cool for 5 minutes, then whisk the ganache until glossy and beginning to thicken. Pour onto the cake and spread over the top and sides, using a palette knife. Leave in a cool place to set; do not refrigerate.

7 Sprinkle the remaining praline on top of the cake to serve.

CHOCOLATE CINNAMON MOUSSE CAKE

Serves 8
Preparation: 25 minutes, plus cooling and decorating
Cooking time: 30–40 minutes
Freezing: not suitable
455 cals per slice

225g (8oz) plain chocolate
125g (4oz) unsalted butter
30ml (2 tbsp) brandy
5 eggs, separated
125g (4oz) caster sugar
5ml (1 tsp) ground cinnamon

TO DECORATE
50g (2oz) plain chocolate
125g (4oz) strawberries
125g (4oz) plain or milk chocolate, for the curls
125g (4oz) white chocolate, for the curls
icing sugar, for dusting

1 Preheat the oven to 160°C/325°F/gas 3. Grease and line a 23cm (9 inch) spring-release cake tin.

2 Break up the chocolate and place in a heatproof bowl over a pan of simmering water. Add the butter and leave until melted. Remove from the heat, add the brandy and stir until smooth.

3 Place the egg yolks in a bowl with 75g (3oz) of the sugar. Whisk until the mixture is pale and thick enough to leave a thin trail on the surface when the whisk is lifted from the bowl. Stir in the melted chocolate mixture.

4 In a separate bowl, whisk the egg whites until stiff. Gradually whisk in the remaining sugar, adding the cinnamon with the final addition of sugar. Using a large metal spoon, fold a quarter of the egg whites into the chocolate mixture to loosen it, then carefully fold in the remainder.

5 Turn the mixture into the prepared tin. Bake for 30–40 minutes until well risen and the centre feels just spongy when gently pressed. Leave to cool in the tin.

6 Transfer the cake to a serving plate, peeling away the lining paper. For the decoration, break up the chocolate and melt in a heatproof bowl set over a pan of simmering water. Dip the strawberries in the chocolate so they are half-coated, letting the excess drip back into the bowl. Place the dipped fruits on a sheet of greaseproof paper to set.

7 Meanwhile, make the chocolate curls. Break the dark and white chocolate into pieces and put into separate heatproof bowls. Place over pans of gently simmering water and leave until melted. Spread alternate lines of dark and white chocolate to a depth of about 5mm (¼ inch) on a marble slab or clean, smooth work surface. When only just set, draw a fine-bladed knife across the chocolate at an angle of 45°.

8 Casually pile the chocolate curls and strawberries onto the cake and dust lightly with icing sugar to serve.

TOP TIP
Undecorated, the cake will keep well in the refrigerator for 2–3 days. Leave at room temperature for 30 minutes before serving.

CHOCOLATE, ALMOND AND SWEET POTATO LOAF

Makes 8–10 slices
Preparation: 20 minutes
Cooking time: 1–1¼ hours
Freezing: suitable
435–350 cals per slice

225g (8oz) sweet potatoes

75g (3oz) flaked almonds

125g (4oz) milk chocolate

125g (4oz) soft margarine

125g (4oz) light muscovado sugar

5ml (1 tsp) vanilla essence

2 eggs

160g (5½oz) self-raising white flour

15g (½oz) cocoa powder

5ml (1 tsp) ground mixed spice

2.5ml (½ tsp) bicarbonate of soda

30ml (2 tbsp) milk

icing sugar, for dusting

1 Peel the sweet potatoes and cut into chunks. Add to a pan of cold water, bring to the boil and cook for 15 minutes or until softened. Drain well and mash with a potato masher.

2 Preheat the oven to 160°C/325°F/gas 3. Grease a 900g (2lb) loaf tin and line the base and long sides with a strip of greaseproof paper. Lightly toast the flaked almonds. Roughly chop the chocolate.

3 Put the margarine, sugar, vanilla essence and eggs in a bowl. Sift the flour, cocoa powder, mixed spice and bicarbonate of soda into the bowl. Add the milk and beat well until smooth and creamy.

4 Stir in the mashed sweet potato, chopped chocolate and 50g (2oz) of the toasted almonds. Turn the mixture into the prepared tin and level the surface. Sprinkle with the remaining almonds.

5 Bake for about 1–1¼ hours until well risen and just firm to the touch. Leave in the tin for 10 minutes, then transfer to a wire rack to cool. Serve dusted with icing sugar.

TOP TIP

Cook this cake as soon as you have mixed it, as the bicarbonate of soda is activated on blending.

CHOCOLATE PECAN FUDGE CAKE

Makes 16 slices
Preparation: 50 minutes, plus cooling
Cooking time: 25 minutes
Freezing: suitable (stage 2)
590 cals per slice

175g (6oz) self-raising white flour

50g (2oz) cocoa powder

10ml (2 tsp) baking powder

175g (6oz) butter or margarine, softened

175g (6oz) caster sugar

4 eggs

10ml (2 tsp) vanilla essence

FILLING
300ml (½ pint) double cream

125g (4oz) shelled pecans

90ml (6 tbsp) maple syrup

ICING
300g (10oz) plain chocolate

50g (2oz) unsalted butter

60ml (4 tbsp) milk

225g (8oz) icing sugar

TO DECORATE
200g (7oz) plain chocolate

cocoa powder, for dusting

1 Preheat the oven to 180°C/350°F/gas 4. Grease and base-line three 19–20 cm (7½–8 inch) sandwich tins.

2 Sift the flour, cocoa and baking powder into a bowl. Add the butter or margarine, sugar, eggs and vanilla essence. Beat, using an electric whisk, for 2 minutes until smooth and paler in colour. Divide the mixture between the prepared tins and level the surfaces. Bake for 25 minutes until risen and just firm to the touch. Turn out onto a wire rack to cool.

3 For the filling, whip the cream until just peaking. Roughly chop the pecans. Place one cake on a serving plate and spread with a quarter of the cream. Scatter with half of the nuts, then drizzle with half of the maple syrup. Spread carefully with another quarter of the cream and position the second cake on top. Cover with the remaining cream, nuts and syrup, then top with the remaining cake.

4 To make the icing, break up the chocolate and place in a saucepan with the butter and milk. Heat gently until the chocolate is melted, stirring frequently. Remove from the heat and beat in the icing sugar until evenly combined. Leave to cool, then swirl over the top and sides of the cake with a palette knife.

5 To make the chocolate curls for the decoration, break up the chocolate and place in a heatproof bowl over a pan of hot water. Leave until melted, then spread evenly onto a marble slab or work surface. When just set draw the blade of a knife, held at a 45° angle, across the chocolate to shave off curls.

6 Scatter the chocolate curls over the top of the cake and dust lightly with cocoa powder.

TOP TIP
If the chocolate breaks when you are making curls, it has set too hard and should be left in a warm place for a few minutes before trying again.

CHOCOLATE LEAF GÂTEAU

Makes 14 slices
Preparation: 1½ hours, plus cooling
Cooking time: 30 minutes
Freezing: suitable (stage 4)
560 cals per slice

50g (2oz) unsalted butter
5 eggs
150g (5oz) caster sugar
125g (4oz) plain white flour
25g (1oz) cocoa powder

FILLING
200g (7oz) white chocolate
300ml (½ pint) double cream
75ml (5 tbsp) Cointreau or other orange-flavoured liqueur

ICING
225g (8oz) plain chocolate
225g (8oz) double cream

TO DECORATE
75g (3oz) bitter chocolate
75g (3oz) plain chocolate
75g (3oz) milk chocolate

selection of clean, dry leaves, such as rose, large mint, lemon, geranium and small bay leaves

1 Preheat the oven to 180°C/350°F/gas 4. Grease and line a 23cm (9 inch) spring-release cake tin. Melt the butter in a saucepan; leave to cool slightly.

2 Put the eggs and sugar in a large heatproof bowl standing over a pan of hot water. Whisk until pale and creamy, and thick enough to leave a trail on the surface when the whisk is lifted.

3 Remove from the heat and whisk until cool. Sift together the flour and cocoa powder, then fold half into the egg mixture using a metal spoon. Pour the butter around the edge of the mixture and lightly fold in. Gradually fold in the remaining flour and cocoa powder.

4 Pour into the tin. Bake for about 30 minutes until well risen, just firm to the touch and beginning to shrink from the sides of the tin. Turn out and cool on a wire rack.

5 To make the filling, finely grate the white chocolate. Whip the cream with the liqueur until thickened but not peaking. Fold in the chocolate. Split the sponge horizontally and sandwich together with the cream. Invert onto a wire rack so that the flat base is now the top of the cake.

6 To make the icing, break up the chocolate and place in a heavy-based saucepan with the cream. Heat gently until the chocolate has almost melted. Remove from the heat and stir until smooth and glossy; let cool slightly.

7 Position a large plate or tray under the wire rack holding the cake. Pour the icing onto the cake. Using a palette knife, ease the icing down the sides until the cake is completely covered. Carefully transfer to a serving plate.

8 For the chocolate leaves, break up the bitter chocolate and place in a heatproof bowl over a pan of hot water and leave until melted. Repeat with the plain and milk chocolate; keep separate.

9 Using a paintbrush, paint the undersides of the leaves with the different melted chocolates, taking it just to the edges. (You'll need about 15 of each shade.) Leave in a cool place or refrigerate until set. Carefully peel the leaves away from the chocolate. Press the chocolate leaves gently around the sides of the gâteau to decorate.

CHOCOLATE AND RASPBERRY TORTE

Makes 12 slices

Preparation: 45 minutes, plus chilling

Cooking time: 12–15 minutes

Freezing: not suitable

375 cals per slice

5 eggs

150g (5oz) caster sugar

125g (4oz) plain white flour

25g (1oz) cocoa powder

FILLING
4 egg yolks

50g (2oz) caster sugar

60ml (4 tbsp) cornflour

10ml (2 tsp) vanilla essence

450ml (¾ pint) milk

90ml (6 tbsp) Grand Marnier or
other orange-flavoured liqueur

300ml (½ pint) double cream

175g (6oz) raspberries

100g (3½oz) plain chocolate,
grated or finely chopped

25g (1oz) preserved stem ginger
in syrup, finely chopped

TO FINISH
cocoa powder, for dusting

1 Grease and line a 23cm (9 inch) spring-release cake tin and a 26 x 16cm (10½ x 6½ inch) shallow rectangular tin. Put the eggs and sugar in a large heatproof bowl set over a pan of hot water. Whisk until the mixture is pale and creamy and leaves a trail when the whisk is lifted from the bowl. Remove from the heat and whisk until cool.

2 Sift the flour and cocoa powder over the mixture, then carefully fold in, using a large metal spoon. Spoon a thin layer of the mixture into the rectangular tin, to give an 8mm (⅜ inch) depth. Turn the remainder into the spring-release tin. Bake both cakes at 200°C/400°C/gas 6 for 12–15 minutes until just firm. Leave to cool.

3 For the filling, beat the egg yolks, sugar, cornflour, vanilla essence and a little of the milk together in a bowl until smooth. Put the remaining milk in a heavy-based pan and bring to the boil, then pour onto the yolk mixture, stirring constantly. Return to the pan and heat gently, stirring until thickened; do not boil. Turn into a bowl, cover the surface closely with a disc of dampened greaseproof paper to prevent a skin forming. Leave to cool for a few minutes.

4 Cut the round cake horizontally into two layers and fit one back into the cleaned tin, cut-side down. Trim off the edges of the rectangular cake, then cut into 4cm (1½ inch) wide strips. Fit these around the side of the tin to make a sponge case. Using a teaspoon, drizzle 45–60ml (3–4 tbsp) of the orange liqueur evenly over both round cake layers.

5 Whip the cream in a bowl until thickened but not peaking. Fold in the cooled custard, raspberries, chocolate, ginger and remaining liqueur. Turn the mixture into the chocolate case and level the surface. Lay the reserved sponge round on top, cut-side up. Chill in the refrigerator overnight.

6 To serve, carefully release the side of the cake tin and invert the chocolate torte onto a large flat plate. Serve dusted with cocoa powder.

RICH CHOCOLATE LACE GÂTEAU

Makes 12 slices
Preparation: 40 minutes, plus chilling
Cooking time: 30 minutes
Freezing: not suitable
495 cals per slice

200g (7oz) plain chocolate, in pieces

175g (6oz) unsalted butter

5 eggs, separated

150g (5oz) light muscovado sugar

5ml (1 tsp) almond essence

75g (3oz) self-raising flour, sifted

125g (4oz) ground almonds

60–75ml (4–5 tbsp) Grand Marnier or other orange-flavoured liqueur

GANACHE
100ml (3½oz) double cream

150g (5oz) plain chocolate, in pieces

TO DECORATE
50g (2oz) plain chocolate

1 Grease and line a 25–26cm (10–10½ inch) round cake tin. Melt the chocolate and butter together in a heatproof bowl over a pan of simmering water; stir until smooth. Beat the egg yolks, sugar and almond essence together in a large bowl until pale and thick. Whisk in the melted chocolate mixture. Carefully fold in the flour and ground almonds, using a large metal spoon.

2 In a separate bowl, whisk the egg whites until stiff. Fold a quarter into the chocolate mixture to lighten it, then fold in the remainder. Turn into the prepared tin and bake at 180°C/350°F/gas 4 for about 30 minutes until risen and just firm. Leave to cool in the tin. Transfer the cake to a large, flat serving plate and drizzle with the liqueur.

3 To make the ganache, pour the cream into a small pan and bring almost to the boil. Remove from the heat and add the chocolate. Leave until melted, then stir until smooth. Transfer to a bowl and leave to cool until slightly thickened. Using a palette knife, spread the ganache over the top and sides of the cake to cover evenly.

4 Measure the circumference of the cake, using a piece of string. Cut a strip of greaseproof paper or non-stick baking parchment the length of the string and 6cm (2½ inches) deep. Melt the chocolate and put into a greaseproof paper icing bag. Snip off the merest tip, then scribble the chocolate randomly and quite heavily all over the paper strip.

5 Carefully lift the strip and secure around the side of the gâteau, so the lower half of the strip touches the side of the cake while the top half stands proud. Carefully place the gâteau in the refrigerator and chill for about 30 minutes until the chocolate has set.

6 Carefully peel away the paper, leaving the chocolate lace collar in position around the side of the cake. Keep the gâteau in a cool place, or chill until required. Serve with softly whipped cream, if desired.

TOP TIP
Don't make the chocolate collar too delicate, otherwise it might break as you remove the paper.

CHOCOLATE CROWN

Makes 12 slices
Preparation: about 1 hour
Cooking time: 50 minutes
Freezing: suitable (stage 2)
665 cals per slice

175g (6oz) self-raising white flour

5ml (1 tsp) baking powder

50g (2oz) cocoa powder

175g (6oz) soft margarine

175g (6oz) caster sugar

3 eggs

TO DECORATE
300ml (½ pint) double cream

300g (10oz) good quality plain chocolate (70% cocoa solids), in pieces

8 Maltesers (optional)

450g (1lb) bought luxury chocolates in paper cases

8 gold wrapped sugared almonds

0.75 metre gold cord

1 Grease and line a deep 18cm (7 inch) round cake tin. Sift the flour, baking powder and cocoa powder into a bowl. Add the margarine, sugar and eggs and beat well for about 2 minutes until smooth and creamy.

2 Turn the mixture into the prepared tin and level the surface. Bake at 170°C/325°F/gas 3 for about 50 minutes until firm. Leave in the tin for 5 minutes, then transfer to a wire rack to cool.

3 To make the chocolate ganache, pour the cream into a heavy-based pan and slowly bring almost to the boil. Remove from the heat and add 200g (7oz) of the chocolate. Leave until melted, then stir until smooth. Transfer the mixture to a bowl and leave until cool and just holding its shape.

4 Cut the cake horizontally into two layers and sandwich together with some of the chocolate cream. Using a sharp knife, trim off the top edge to give a domed centre. Place the cake on a flat plate and spread the top and sides with the reserved chocolate cream, spreading as smoothly as possible.

5 To make the crown, melt the remaining chocolate in a heatproof bowl over a pan of simmering water; set aside. Measure the exact circumference of the cake with a piece of string. Cut two strips of greaseproof paper the length of the string and 10cm (4 inches) wide. Fold one paper strip in half, then in half twice more to make a rectangle of eight thicknesses. Using a pencil, draw a curve between the two folded points, then cut along the curve through all the thicknesses. Open out the paper to reveal the fluted edge and lay on top of the second paper strip. Draw the fluted outline onto the second paper strip; discard the cut paper strip.

6 Put the melted chocolate in a paper piping bag and snip off the tip. Pipe along the fluted edge and down the sides and base of the paper. Scribble diagonal lines all over the strip, within the chocolate border. Scribble more lines across in the opposite direction to create a dense lattice design. (Reserve a little chocolate in the piping bag.) Leave until the chocolate is just sufficiently set that it doesn't run when you pick up the paper. Carefully lift the paper strip, by the uncoated areas, and position around the cake so the chocolate rests against the side of the cake and the ends of the strip just meet. Chill or leave in a cool place until the chocolate has set.

7 Carefully peel away the greaseproof paper, leaving the chocolate collar in position. Pipe a dot of melted chocolate on each of the points of the crown and gently secure a Malteser, if using. (If the chocolate has set in the piping bag, soften in the microwave.) Pile the chocolates and sugared almonds on top of the cake. Secure the gold cord around the base. Store the cake in a cool place until ready to serve.

WARM CHOCOLATE CHEESECAKE

Serves 8
Preparation: 15 minutes
Cooking time: about 1¼ hours
Freezing: not suitable
264 cals per slice

50g (2oz) margarine or butter

50g (2oz) plain flour

50g (2oz) porridge oats

75g (3oz) golden caster sugar

450g (1lb) natural cottage cheese

4 eggs

50g (2oz) cocoa powder

5ml (1 tsp) vanilla essence

25g (1oz) plain chocolate, coarsely grated

1 Lightly grease and line the base of a 20cm (8 inch) non-stick, loose-bottomed cake tin.

2 Put the fat in a saucepan and heat until melted. Remove from the heat and add the flour, oats and 25g (1oz) of the sugar. Mix well together then press the mixture in the base of the prepared tin. Bake in the oven at 180°C/350°F/gas 4 for 10–15 minutes until firm.

3 Meanwhile, rub the cottage cheese through a sieve into a bowl. Beat 2 whole eggs and 2 egg yolks together, then stir into the cottage cheese. Sift in the cocoa powder and add the vanilla essence and remaining sugar. Mix well together.

4 Whisk the remaining 2 egg whites together until stiff then, using a metal spoon, fold into the mixture. Pour the mixture over the base.

5 Bake in the oven at 180°C/350°F/gas 4 for about 1 hour or until firm to the touch and set. Leave to cool for 5 minutes, then carefully remove from the tin. Sprinkle the grated chocolate evenly over the top, and serve while still warm.

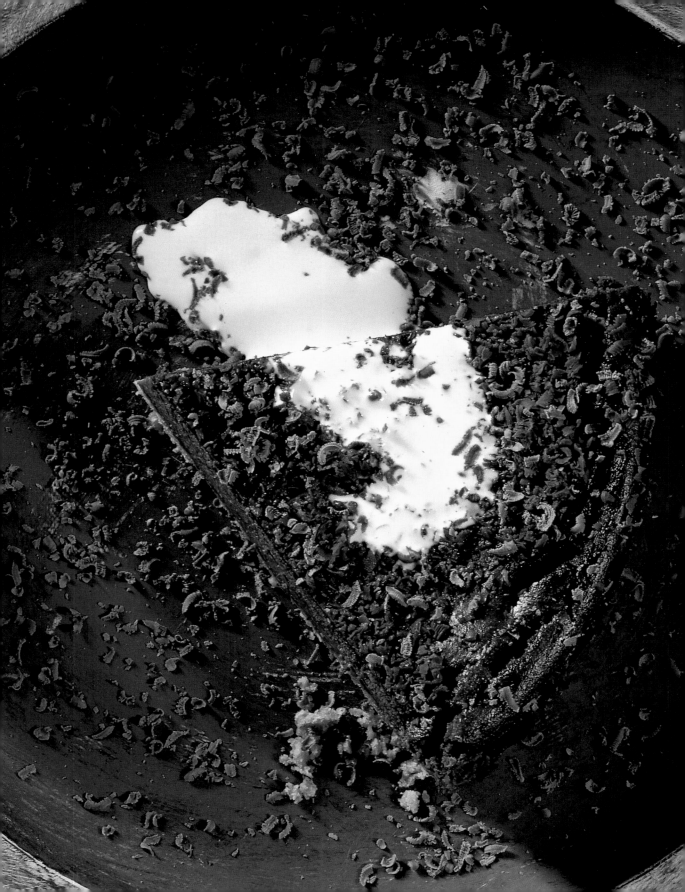

BEST EVERYDAY CAKES

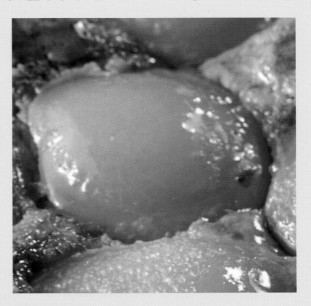

RASPBERRY AND PISTACHIO SANDWICH CAKE

Makes 8–10 slices
Preparation: 20 minutes, plus cooling
Cooking time: 30 minutes
Freezing: suitable (stage 3)
635–510 cals per slice

65g (2½oz) shelled pistachio nuts

225g (8oz) self-raising white flour

10ml (2 tsp) baking powder

4 eggs

225g (8oz) caster sugar

225g (8oz) unsalted butter, softened

5ml (1 tsp) vanilla essence

FILLING
75ml (5 tbsp) raspberry jam

125g (4oz) raspberries

150ml (¼ pint) double cream, or 75ml (5 tbsp) yogurt and 75ml (5 tbsp) cream

TO DECORATE
225g (8oz) raspberries

25g (1oz) pistachio nuts

icing sugar, for dusting (optional)

1 Preheat the oven to 160°C/325°F/gas 3. Grease and base-line two 20cm (8 inch) sandwich tins. Put the pistachio nuts in a bowl and pour on boiling water to cover. Leave for 1 minute, then drain and remove the skins. Finely chop the nuts.

2 Sift the flour and baking powder into a bowl. Add the eggs, sugar, butter and vanilla essence and beat, using an electric whisk, until pale and creamy. Stir in the chopped nuts.

3 Divide the mixture evenly between the tins and level the surfaces. Bake for about 30 minutes until well risen and firm to the touch. Turn out of the tins and leave to cool on a wire rack.

4 Heat the jam in a small pan until just melted; leave to cool. Place one cake layer on a serving plate. Whip the cream until just peaking and spread over the cake. Scatter with the raspberries, then spoon over the melted jam. Top with the second cake layer.

5 To decorate, scatter the raspberries over the cake. Skin the pistachios (as above) and sprinkle over the top. Dust with icing sugar if desired, and keep in a cool place until ready to serve.

TOP TIP
The mixture should be very soft and drop easily from a spoon before baking. If it seems a little stiff, stir in a dash of milk or water.

VARIATION
Replace the pistachio nuts with the scooped-out pulp from 3 passion fruit. Replace the raspberries on top of the cake with wedges of fig and seedless black grapes. Scatter the cake with more passion fruit pulp.

CINNAMON SPONGE WITH BLUEBERRIES

Makes 6 slices
Preparation: 30 minutes, plus cooling
Cooking time: 30 minutes
Freezing: not suitable
235 cals per slice

3 eggs

75g (3oz) caster sugar

15ml (1 tbsp) tepid water

75g (3oz) plain white flour

5ml (1 tsp) ground cinnamon

FILLING
150ml (¼ pint) half-fat double cream

15ml (1 tbsp) icing sugar

60ml (4 tbsp) Greek yogurt

75g (3oz) blueberries, washed and halved

15ml (1 tbsp) chopped fresh mint

TO FINISH
45ml (3 tbsp) redcurrant jelly

150g (5oz) blueberries, washed and dried

15ml (1 tbsp) icing sugar

sprigs of fresh mint, to decorate

1 Grease two 18cm (7 inch) sandwich tins and base-line with non-stick baking parchment.

2 Place the eggs, sugar and water in a large heatproof bowl and place over a saucepan of hot water. Whisk for 6–7 minutes until very thick and mousse-like. Remove from the heat and continue whisking for 5 minutes or until cool.

3 Sift the flour and cinnamon together and carefully fold into the mousse mixture. Turn into the tins and spread the mixture evenly with a spatula. Bake at 180°C/350°F/gas 4 for 25 minutes. Allow to stand in the tins for 5 minutes, then turn onto a wire rack to cool completely.

4 To make the filling, whip the cream with the icing sugar to form soft peaks. Fold in the yogurt, blueberries and mint and use to sandwich the cakes together.

5 To finish, warm the redcurrant jelly in a small pan, add the blueberries and coat well. Spoon the blueberry mixture on top of the cake, dust with icing sugar and decorate with sprigs of mint.

CRUMBLY APPLE AND CHEESE CAKE

Makes 10 slices
Preparation: 20 minutes
Cooking time: 50 minutes–1 hour
Freezing: suitable
345 cals per slice

575g (1¼lb) dessert apples
50g (2oz) brazil nuts
175g (6oz) self-raising white flour
5ml (1 tsp) baking powder
75g (3oz) light muscovado sugar
50g (2oz) raisins
50g (2oz) sultanas
2 eggs
90ml (3fl oz) sunflower oil
225g (8oz) Caerphilly cheese

TO FINISH
icing sugar, for sprinkling

1 Preheat the oven to 180°C/350°F/gas 4. Grease a 5cm (2 inch) deep, 23cm (9 inch) round loose-based flan tin. Peel, core and thinly slice the apples. Roughly chop the nuts.

2 Sift the flour and baking powder into a bowl. Stir in the sugar, raisins, sultanas, nuts and apples, and mix until evenly combined. Beat the eggs with the oil and add to the dry ingredients. Stir until all the flour mixture is moistened and evenly incorporated.

3 Turn half the mixture into the prepared tin and level the surface. Crumble the cheese over the surface, then cover with the remaining cake mixture. Roughly spread the mixture to the edges of the tin.

4 Bake for 50 minutes to 1 hour until golden and just firm. Leave to cool in the tin for 10 minutes, then transfer to a wire rack. Serve warm, sprinkled with icing sugar.

TOP TIP
Do not smooth the second layer of cake mixture too neatly; a rough surface gives a more interesting finish.

VARIATION
Replace the Caerphilly with a similar cheese, such as Wensleydale or Lancashire.

RIPPLED DATE AND BANANA LOAF

Makes 8–10 slices
Preparation: 20 minutes
Cooking time: 1¼–1½ hours
Freezing: suitable
495–395 cals per slice

250g (9oz) stoned dried dates

grated rind and juice of 1 lemon

2 ripe bananas

175g (6oz) unsalted butter, softened

175g (6oz) caster sugar

3 eggs

225g (8oz) self-raising white flour

2.5ml (½ tsp) baking powder

1 Preheat the oven to 160°C/325°F/gas 3. Grease and line a 1.1 litre (2 pint) loaf tin. Set aside 4 dates. Place the remainder in a small heavy-based saucepan and add the lemon rind and juice, and 90ml (3fl oz) water. Bring to the boil, reduce the heat and simmer gently for 5 minutes until the dates are soft and pulpy. Purée the mixture in a food processor or blender until smooth. (Alternatively mash together in a bowl, using a fork.)

2 Mash the bananas until completely smooth. Cream the butter and sugar together in a bowl until pale and fluffy. Add the banana purée and eggs. Sift the flour and baking powder into the bowl and beat together until thoroughly combined.

3 Spoon a third of the banana mixture into the prepared tin and level the surface. Spread half of the date purée over the surface. Repeat these layers, then cover with the remaining banana mixture.

4 Cut the reserved dates into thin lengths and scatter them over the surface. Bake for 1–1¼ hours until well risen and firm to the touch. Leave in the tin for 15 minutes, then transfer to a wire rack to cool. Store in an airtight container for up to 1 week.

TOP TIP
The date purée needs to be similar in consistency to the banana mixture. If it is too thick, beat in a little water.

VARIATION
Add 2.5ml (½ tsp) ground cinnamon or 25g (1oz) toasted sunflower seeds to the banana mixture.

ALMOND AND APRICOT ROULADE

Makes 8 slices
Preparation: 20 minutes, plus standing
Cooking time: 20 minutes
Freezing: not suitable
380 cals per slice

ROULADE
25g (1oz) flaked almonds

5 eggs, separated

150g (5oz) caster sugar

5ml (1 tsp) vanilla essence

125g (4oz) white almond paste, grated

45ml (3 tbsp) plain flour

45ml (3 tbsp) amaretto liqueur

FILLING
6 ripe apricots

300g (10oz) crème fraîche

TO FINISH
caster or icing sugar, for dusting

1 Preheat the oven to 180°C/350°F/gas 4. Grease a 33 x 23cm (13 x 9 inches) Swiss roll tin and line with greased non-stick baking parchment. Scatter the flaked almonds evenly over the paper.

2 Whisk the egg yolks with 125g (4oz) of the sugar until pale and fluffy. Stir in the vanilla essence and grated almond paste. Sift the flour over the mixture, then lightly fold in.

3 Whisk the egg whites in another bowl, until stiff but not dry. Gradually whisk in the remaining sugar. Using a large metal spoon, carefully fold a quarter of the egg whites into the almond mixture to loosen, then fold in the remainder.

4 Turn into the prepared tin and gently ease the mixture into the corners. Bake for about 20 minutes or until well risen and just firm to the touch. Remove from the oven and cover with a sheet of non-stick baking parchment and a damp tea-towel. Leave until cool, or overnight if possible.

5 Remove the tea-towel and invert the roulade (and paper) onto a baking sheet. Peel off the lining paper. Sprinkle another piece of baking parchment with caster sugar and flip the roulade onto it. Drizzle with the amaretto liqueur.

6 Halve and stone the apricots, then cut into small pieces. Spread the roulade with the crème fraîche and scatter with the apricots. Starting at one of the narrow ends, roll up the roulade. Transfer to a plate and dust with caster or icing sugar to serve.

TOP TIP
Don't worry if the roulade cracks during rolling – this is a natural characteristic.

VARIATIONS
Replace the apricots with strawberries or raspberries. Brandy or an orange-flavoured liqueur can be used instead of the amaretto.

WALNUT TORTE

Makes 8–10 slices
Preparation: 25 minutes, plus cooling
Cooking time: 30 minutes
Freezing: not suitable
530–425 cals per slice

165g (5½oz) walnuts

150g (5oz) unsalted butter

150g (5oz) caster sugar

5 eggs, separated

grated rind of 1 orange

150g (5oz) ricotta cheese

40g (1½oz) plain white flour

TO FINISH
90ml (6 tbsp) apricot jam

10ml (2 tsp) orange juice

25g (1oz) bitter chocolate, in one piece (at room temperature)

1 Preheat the oven to 190°C/375°F/gas 5. Grease and base-line a 23cm (9 inch) spring-release cake tin. Lightly toast the walnuts and allow to cool. Roughly chop 125g (4oz) of the walnuts; chop the remainder finely and set aside for the decoration.

2 Cream the butter and 125g (4oz) of the sugar together in a bowl until pale and fluffy. Add the egg yolks, orange rind, ricotta cheese, flour and roughly chopped walnuts. Mix gently until evenly combined.

3 Put the egg whites into another large bowl and whisk until stiff but not dry. Gradually whisk in the remaining sugar. Using a large metal spoon, fold a quarter into the cheese mixture to loosen it slightly, then carefully fold in the remaining egg whites.

4 Turn the mixture into the prepared tin and gently level the surface. Bake for about 30 minutes until risen and just firm. Remove from the oven and leave to cool in the tin.

5 Heat the apricot jam in a pan until melted, then press through a sieve into a bowl and stir in the orange juice to make a glaze. Brush half around the side of the cake. Using a palette knife, coat the side of the cake with the finely chopped walnuts.

6 Brush the remaining glaze over the top of the cake. Using a swivel vegetable peeler, shave curls from the chocolate and scatter over the top of the cake to serve.

TOP TIP
This gâteau can be made in advance and kept in the refrigerator for up to 2 days.

VARIATION
Omit the chocolate curls. Cover the top of the cake with halved and stoned greengages or small plums. Glaze the fruit with 60ml (4 tbsp) warmed and sieved greengage or plum jam.

FROSTED LIME SPONGE

Makes 10 slices
Preparation: 20 minutes
Cooking time: 20–25 minutes
Freezing: suitable (stage 5)
465 cals per slice

175g (6oz) unsalted butter or
margarine, softened

175g (6oz) caster sugar

finely grated rind of 2 limes

3 medium eggs, lightly beaten

175g (6oz) self-raising white flour

TO FINISH
300g (10oz) full-fat cream cheese

30–45ml (2–3 tbsp) lime juice
(1½–2 limes)

125g (4oz) icing sugar, sifted

lime rind, to decorate

1 Grease two 18cm (7 inch) sandwich tins and dust with flour, shaking out the excess.

2 Beat the butter or margarine, sugar and lime rind together in a bowl until very pale and creamy.

3 Add the eggs gradually, beating well after each addition, and adding a little of the flour if the mixture starts to curdle.

4 Sift the flour over the mixture, then fold in using a large metal spoon.

5 Divide the mixture between the tins and level the surface. Bake at 180°C/350°F/gas 4 for 20–25 minutes until risen and just firm to the touch. Transfer to a wire rack and leave to cool.

6 To make the frosting, beat the cream cheese in a bowl to soften. Add the lime juice and icing sugar and beat until smooth and creamy.

7 Sandwich the cakes together with about half of the frosting and place on a serving plate. Using a palette knife, spread the rest of the cream cheese frosting over the top. Decorate with strips of lime rind. Store in a cool place and eat within 1–2 days.

VARIATION
Flavour the cake mixture with the grated rind of 1 large orange instead of the lime rind, and use orange juice rather than lime juice for the glaze.

LAVENDER MADEIRA CAKE

Makes 10 slices
Preparation: 20 minutes
Cooking time: 50 minutes
Freezing: suitable
370 cals per slice

3 fresh (or dried) lavender sprigs
225g (8oz) self-raising white flour
5ml (1 tsp) baking powder
finely grated rind of 1 lemon
175g (6oz) unsalted butter,
softened
175g (6oz) caster sugar
3 eggs
ICING
3 sprigs fresh (or dried) lavender
175g (6oz) icing sugar
15ml (1 tbsp) lemon juice
10–15ml (2–3 tsp) water

TO DECORATE
lavender sprigs (optional)

1 Grease a 900g (2lb) loaf tin. Line the base and long sides with one continuous strip of paper, which overhangs the edges so the cake can easily be lifted out of the tin. Line the ends of the tin with more paper.

2 Remove the lavender flowers from their stalks. Sift the flour and baking powder into a mixing bowl.

3 Add the lemon rind, lavender, softened butter, sugar and eggs to the flour and beat well until the mixture is smooth and creamy.

4 Turn the mixture into the prepared tin and level the surface. Bake at 180°C/350°F/gas 4 for 30 minutes, then lower the setting to 170°C/325°F/gas 3. Bake for a further 20 minutes or until firm and a skewer inserted into the centre comes out clean. Leave to cool in the tin.

5 To make the icing, strip the lavender flowers from their stalks and put them in a bowl with the icing sugar, lemon juice and 10ml (2 tsp) of the water. Mix until smooth. The icing should thickly coat the back of a spoon. Add a little extra water if it is too stiff.

6 Pour the icing evenly over the cake and leave to set. Serve sliced, decorated with extra lavender, if liked.

BRAZIL NUT AND POLENTA CAKE

Makes 10 slices
Preparation: 15 minutes
Cooking time: about 50 minutes
Freezing: suitable
380 cals per slice

150g (5oz) brazil nuts

150g (5oz) unsalted butter, softened

150g (5oz) light muscovado sugar

2 eggs, lightly beaten

125g (4oz) plain white flour, plus an extra 15ml (1 tbsp)

5ml (1 tsp) baking powder

5ml (1 tsp) ground allspice

75ml (3fl oz) milk

65g (2½oz) instant polenta

60ml (4 tbsp) clear honey or maple syrup

1 Grease and line an 18cm (7 inch) square, deep cake tin. Cut half of the brazil nuts in half and set aside for the topping. Roughly chop the rest.

2 Cream the butter and sugar together in a bowl until light and fluffy. Gradually add the eggs, beating well after each addition.

3 Sift the 125g (4oz) flour with the baking powder and allspice into the bowl, then fold in using a large metal spoon. Add the milk, polenta and chopped brazil nuts; fold in until evenly mixed.

4 Turn into the prepared tin and level the surface. Dip the halved nuts in flour and arrange around the edge of the mixture. Bake at 180°C/350°F/gas 4 for about 50 minutes until risen and just firm in the centre.

5 Leave the cake in the tin for 5 minutes, then transfer to a wire rack to cool. Drizzle with the honey to glaze.

> TOP TIP
> The cake can be stored, wrapped in greaseproof paper, in an airtight tin for 4–5 days.

CHERRY, LEMON AND ALMOND CAKE

Makes 18 slices
Preparation: 20 minutes, plus cooling
Cooking time: about 50 minutes
Freezing: suitable
335 cals per slice

300g (10oz) natural glacé cherries, rinsed and dried

150g (5oz) self-raising white flour, plus an extra 15ml (1 tbsp)

250g (9oz) unsalted butter, softened

250g (9oz) caster sugar

finely grated rind of 2 lemons

5 eggs, separated

150g (5oz) ground almonds

45ml (3 tbsp) milk

25g (1oz) slivered or flaked almonds

GLAZE
100g (3½oz) caster sugar

juice of 2 lemons

5ml (1 tsp) almond essence

1 Grease and line a 23cm (9 inch) square cake tin. Halve the cherries and toss in 15ml (1 tbsp) flour. Cream the butter and sugar together in a bowl until light and fluffy. Stir in the lemon rind and egg yolks.

2 Sift the flour into the bowl. Add the ground almonds and milk and fold in, using a large metal spoon. Whisk the egg whites in a clean bowl until peaking; fold a quarter into the creamed mixture to lighten it, then carefully fold in the remainder.

3 Turn the mixture into the prepared tin. Scatter over the cherries and almonds. Bake at 180°C/350°F/gas 4 for about 50 minutes until golden and just firm.

4 For the glaze, put the sugar in a small, heavy-based saucepan with 100ml (3½fl oz) water and heat gently until dissolved. Bring to the boil, add the lemon juice and almond essence and boil rapidly for 5 minutes until syrupy. Leave to cool, then spoon over the cake. Store in an airtight container for up to 5 days.

COFFEE AND PECAN LAYER CAKE

Makes 10 slices
Preparation: 30 minutes, plus cooling
Cooking time: 20–25 minutes
Freezing: suitable (stage 2)
570 cals per slice

175g (6oz) self-raising white flour

7.5ml (1½ tsp) baking powder

175g (6oz) unsalted butter, softened

175g (6oz) light muscovado sugar

3 eggs

30ml (2 tbsp) instant coffee, dissolved in 15ml (1 tbsp) hot water

100g (3½oz) pecan halves, chopped

FILLING
75g (3oz) unsalted butter, softened

175g (6oz) icing sugar

2.5ml (½ tsp) vanilla essence

FROSTING
225g (8oz) caster sugar

pinch of cream of tartar

1 large egg white

15ml (1 tbsp) instant coffee, dissolved in 10ml (2 tsp) hot water

TO DECORATE
pecan halves

1 Grease and base-line three 18cm (7 inch) sandwich tins. Sift the flour and baking powder into a bowl. Add the butter, sugar, eggs and coffee mixture and whisk until pale and creamy. Stir in the pecans.

2 Divide between the prepared tins and level the surfaces. Bake at 180°C/350°F/gas 4 for 20–25 minutes until just firm to the touch. Transfer to a wire rack and leave to cool.

3 To make the filling, beat the butter, icing sugar and vanilla essence together in a bowl with 5ml (1 tsp) boiling water until pale and creamy. Use to sandwich the cake layers on a serving plate.

4 To make the frosting, heat the sugar and cream of tartar in a small, heavy-based saucepan with 60ml (4 tbsp) water until dissolved. Bring to the boil and boil, without stirring, until 116°C/240°F is registered on a sugar thermometer.

5 Meanwhile, whisk the egg white in a bowl until stiff. Pour on the sugar syrup in a thin stream, whisking all the time until the frosting is glossy and peaking. Stir in the coffee. Spread the frosting over the top and sides of the cake. Decorate with pecan halves.

LEMON AND HAZELNUT CAKE

Makes 8 slices
Preparation: 50 minutes, plus cooling
Cooking time: 25 minutes
Freezing: suitable (stage 3)
370 cals per slice

1 unwaxed ripe, juicy lemon

125g (4oz) ground hazelnuts

75g (3oz) plain white flour

5ml (1 tsp) baking powder

150g (5oz) caster sugar

4 eggs

TO FINISH
90ml (6 tbsp) lemon curd

150ml (¼ pint) double cream, whipped

icing sugar, for dusting

1 Grease and base-line two 20cm (8 inch) sandwich tins. Put the whole lemon in a small saucepan and add sufficient hot water to just cover. Simmer gently for about 45 minutes until very tender. Drain, reserving 45ml (3 tbsp) of the juice. Quarter the lemon and remove the pips, then place in a food processor with the reserved juice and process until almost smooth.

2 Mix together the ground hazelnuts, flour, baking powder and 50g (2oz) of the sugar. Put the remaining sugar in a heatproof bowl with the eggs and beat over a pan of simmering water until the whisk leaves a trail when lifted from the bowl. Fold in the hazelnut mixture and lemon purée.

3 Divide the mixture between the prepared tins and level the surfaces. Bake at 170°C/325°F/gas 3 for about 25 minutes until risen and just firm. Transfer to a wire rack to cool.

4 Sandwich the cakes together with the lemon curd and whipped cream. Serve generously dusted with icing sugar.

ICED ROSEMARY CAKE

Makes 12 slices
Preparation: 20 minutes, plus cooling
Cooking time: about 1 hour
Freezing: suitable (stage 3)
325 cals per slice

3 tender fresh rosemary sprigs,
each about 10cm (4 inches), stalks
removed

175g (6oz) unsalted butter,
softened

175g (6oz) caster sugar

10ml (2 tsp) vanilla essence

3 eggs, beaten

225g (8oz) self-raising white flour

30ml (2 tbsp) milk

GLAZE
225g (8oz) icing sugar

finely grated rind of ½ orange

15ml (1 tbsp) orange juice

TO DECORATE
rosemary sprigs

1 Grease and line a 15cm (6 inch) round cake tin. Finely chop the rosemary leaves and put half in a bowl with the butter and sugar. Beat until pale and creamy. Stir in the vanilla essence.

2 Gradually beat in the eggs, a little at a time, adding a little of the flour to prevent curdling. Sift the remaining flour into the bowl. Add the milk and fold in.

3 Turn into the prepared tin and level the surface. Bake at 180°C/350°F/gas 4 for 50 minutes to 1 hour until firm and a skewer inserted in the centre comes out clean.

4 Meanwhile, put the remaining chopped rosemary in a small saucepan with 30ml (2 tbsp) water. Heat gently for 2 minutes to infuse the water with the rosemary; leave to cool.

5 Sift the icing sugar into a bowl and add the orange rind and juice. Strain the rosemary juice into the bowl and mix to the consistency of pouring cream, adding a little more water if necessary.

6 Leave the cake to cool for 5 minutes, then run a knife between the cake and the lining paper. Pour the icing over the cake and leave to cool completely before removing the paper. Decorate with rosemary sprigs.

CHERRY AND APPLE STREUSEL

Makes 10 slices
Preparation: 30 minutes, plus cooling
Cooking time: about 50 minutes
Freezing: suitable
405 cals per slice

225g (8oz) self-raising white flour

finely grated rind of 1 lemon

175g (6oz) unsalted butter

150g (5oz) light muscovado sugar

75g (3oz) ground almonds

1 egg

FILLING
5 tart juicy dessert apples,
preferably Cox's

40g (1½oz) butter

425g (15oz) can pitted black
cherries

5ml (1 tsp) cornflour

5ml (1 tsp) vanilla essence

juice of ½ lemon

TO FINISH
icing sugar, for dusting

1 Lightly grease a 23cm (9 inch) spring-release cake tin. For the filling, peel, core and roughly dice the apples. Melt the butter in a frying pan and gently fry the apples for about 3 minutes until softened.

2 Drain the cherries, reserving 60ml (2fl oz) juice. Blend the reserved juice with the cornflour in a separate pan. Add the vanilla essence and lemon juice; bring to the boil. Add the cherries and cook for 1 minute until thickened. Leave to cool.

3 Put the flour and lemon rind in a food processor. Add the butter, cut into small pieces, and blend until the mixture starts to stick together. Add the sugar and ground almonds and blend until crumbly. (Alternatively, rub the butter into the flour by hand, then stir in the sugar and almonds.)

4 Reserve 175g (6oz) of the mixture. Add the egg to the remainder and mix to a dough. Turn into the prepared tin, packing the mixture firmly onto the base and 2.5cm (1 inch) up the sides to make a case. Use a metal spoon to level the mixture.

5 Stir the apples into the cherry mixture and spoon into the case. Scatter with the crumble. Bake at 180°C/350°F/gas 4 for about 50 minutes until slightly risen and pale golden. Cool in the tin, then serve dusted with icing sugar.

APRICOT AND WALNUT SHORTCAKE

Makes 8 slices
Preparation: 15 minutes, plus cooling
Cooking time: 30–35 minutes
Freezing: not suitable
360 cals per slice

175g (6oz) self-raising white flour

2.5ml (½ tsp) ground cinnamon

75g (3oz) unsalted butter, softened

50g (2oz) caster sugar

1 egg

FILLING
100g (3½oz) broken walnuts

100g (3½oz) caster sugar

1 egg white

410g (14½oz) can apricot halves in natural juice

45ml (3 tbsp) apricot jam, sieved

1 Grease a shallow 20cm (8 inch) spring-release cake tin. Put the flour and cinnamon in a food processor with the butter and blend until the mixture resembles fine crumbs. Add the sugar and egg; mix to a soft dough.

2 Turn into the prepared tin and pack into an even layer using the back of a spoon.

3 Process the walnuts until finely ground. Add the sugar and egg white and blend to a soft paste. Spread the mixture over the shortcake to 1cm (½ inch) from the edge.

4 Thoroughly drain the apricots and pat dry, reserving 60ml (4 tbsp) of the juice. Arrange them, cut-sides down, over the filling. Bake at 180°C/350°F/gas 4 for 30–35 minutes until risen and just firm.

5 Put the jam and apricot juice in a small pan and bring to the boil. Cook for about 2 minutes until syrupy. Spread this glaze on top of the shortcake. Serve warm or cold.

VARIATION
Use ground almonds instead of the walnuts and stoned fresh or canned plums instead of the apricots.

PISTACHIO ANGEL CAKE

Makes 12 slices
Preparation: 25 minutes, plus cooling
Cooking time: 35–40 minutes
Freezing: not suitable
340 cals per slice

75g (3oz) pistachio nuts

7 egg whites

1.25ml (¼ tsp) salt

5ml (1 tsp) cream of tartar

5ml (1 tsp) almond essence

275g (10oz) caster sugar

175g (6oz) plain white flour

FROSTING
250g (9oz) mascarpone cheese

10ml (2 tsp) lemon juice

120ml (4fl oz) coconut milk

125g (4oz) icing sugar

TO DECORATE
pistachio nuts

1 Oil a 1.7 litre (3 pint) ring mould, then dust with flour, shaking out the excess. Soak the nuts in boiling water for 3 minutes. Drain, remove the skins by rubbing between layers of kitchen paper, then chop finely.

2 Whisk the egg whites in a large bowl until foamy. Add the salt and cream of tartar and whisk until stiff. Add the almond essence.

3 Gradually add the sugar, whisking well after each addition. Sift the flour over the mixture and fold in, using a large metal spoon. Fold in the nuts.

4 Turn into the ring mould and bake at 170°C/325°F/gas 3 for 35–40 minutes or until firm, and a skewer inserted into the centre comes out clean. Invert onto a wire rack but do not remove the tin. Leave to cool, then loosen and remove the tin.

5 To make the frosting, whisk together the mascarpone, lemon juice, coconut milk and icing sugar until smooth; chill until thickened. Transfer the cake to a serving plate and spread with the frosting. Scatter over pistachio nuts to decorate.

BUTTERSCOTCH NUT GÂTEAU

Makes 12 slices
Preparation: 35 minutes, plus cooling
Cooking time: about 15 minutes
Freezing: not suitable
580 cals per slice

125g (4oz) brazil nuts
5 eggs
150g (5oz) caster sugar
150g (5oz) plain white flour

FILLING
100g (3½oz) unsalted butter
200g (7oz) dark muscovado sugar
45ml (3 tbsp) cornflour
300ml (½ pint) milk
600ml (1 pint) double cream
10ml (2 tsp) vanilla essence

1 Set aside 12 nuts for decoration; finely chop the remainder. Line three baking sheets with non-stick paper and draw a 25cm (10 inch) circle on each. Grease the circles.

2 Whisk the eggs and sugar in a heatproof bowl over a pan of hot water until thick and pale, and the whisk leaves a trail when lifted. Remove from the heat and whisk until cool.

3 Sift the flour over the mixture. Add the chopped nuts and fold in, using a large metal spoon. Spread the mixture over the marked circles. Bake at 180°C/350°F/gas 4 for 15 minutes or until just firm. Leave to cool.

4 Melt the butter in a pan, add the sugar and stir until dissolved, then boil for 1 minute. Add 50ml (2fl oz) boiling water; stir until smooth.

5 Blend the cornflour with a little of the milk. Put the remaining milk in a saucepan with 150ml (¼ pint) of the cream and bring to the boil. Pour over the cornflour mixture, stirring. Add to the butter mixture and cook, stirring, until thickened and smooth. Transfer to a bowl and leave to cool. Set aside 45ml (3 tbsp) for decoration.

6 Trim the sponges to 25cm (10 inch) rounds. Dampen and line the sides of a 25cm (10 inch) loose-bottomed cake tin with greaseproof paper. Place one cake layer in the tin.

7 Whip the remaining cream in a bowl with the vanilla essence until holding its shape. Spread half over the sponge in the tin. Cover with a third of the butterscotch mixture. Repeat these layers then top up with the final sponge and the remaining butterscotch. Chill in the refrigerator for at least 2 hours to firm up.

8 Carefully unmould the gâteau and transfer to a serving plate. Arrange the reserved nuts around the edge. Using a piping bag fitted with a plain nozzle, drizzle the reserved butterscotch on top of the gâteau. Chill until ready to serve.

WALNUT CAKE WITH CRÈME ANGLAISE

Serves 6–8
Preparation: 45 minutes
Cooking time: 1 hour
Freezing: suitable
705–530 cals per serving

150g (5oz) unsalted butter, softened

125g (4oz) caster sugar

4 eggs, separated

finely grated rind of 1 lemon

90ml (6 tbsp) fine dry brown breadcrumbs

150g (5oz) walnuts

CRÈME ANGLAISE
300ml (½ pint) milk

15ml (1 tbsp) caster sugar

1 vanilla pod, split

2 egg yolks, beaten

30ml (2 tbsp) brandy

CARAMEL SYRUP
125g (4oz) caster sugar

TO DECORATE
8–12 walnut halves

1 Preheat the oven to 170°C/325°F/gas 3. Brush a 23cm (9 inch) spring-release cake tin with melted butter, allow to set, then dust out with flour. Line the base with non-stick baking parchment.

2 In a bowl, cream the butter with 75g (3oz) sugar until pale and creamy. Beat in the egg yolks, one at a time, then the lemon rind and breadcrumbs.

3 Finely grind the walnuts in a blender or food processor; do not over-process or they will become oily. Fold into the egg mixture.

4 In another bowl, whisk the egg whites until stiff but not dry. Whisk in the remaining sugar, until stiff and shiny. Gently fold into the cake mixture. Spoon into the cake tin, level the surface and bake for about 1 hour until risen and firm to the touch. To test, insert a skewer into the centre – it should come out clean. Remove from the tin and leave to cool on a wire rack.

5 To make the crème anglaise, put the milk, sugar and vanilla pod in a saucepan and bring almost to the boil. Set aside to infuse for 15 minutes. Remove the vanilla pod. Pour onto the egg yolks, whisking. Return to the pan and stir over a low heat until thickened enough to coat the back of a wooden spoon. Pour into a cold bowl and stir in the brandy. Cover, cool and then chill.

6 For the caramel sauce, put the sugar in a heavy-based saucepan with 30ml (2 tbsp) water. Heat gently to dissolve, then boil steadily to a deep golden brown caramel. Remove from the heat and carefully add 90ml (6 tbsp) cold water; it will splutter and harden. Stir over a low heat until melted, then boil until syrupy. Dip the walnuts into the caramel, turning to coat them.

7 To serve, pool a little custard on each serving plate and place a thin slice of cake on top. Decorate with the walnuts and drizzle with caramel.

WALNUT AND HONEY CAKE

Serves 6–8
Preparation: 25 minutes
Cooking time: 1–1¼ hours
Freezing: suitable
568–426 cals per slice

125g (4oz) butter

125g (4oz) caster sugar

3 eggs, beaten

125g (4oz) self-raising wholemeal flour

5ml (1 tsp) baking powder

60ml (4 tbsp) clear honey

finely grated rind and juice of 1 lemon

175g (6oz) walnuts, coarsely chopped

1 Grease and line a 1kg (2lb) loaf tin. Beat together the butter and sugar until very light and fluffy. Beat in the eggs a little at a time, beating well after each addition. Mix together the flour and baking powder and fold into the creamed mixture.

2 Stir in the honey, lemon rind and juice, and all but 30ml (2 tbsp) of the walnuts. Spoon into the prepared tin and spread the mixture evenly.

3 Bake in the oven at 180°C/350°F/gas 4 for about 30–40 minutes. Scatter the reserved walnuts over the surface and cook for a further 30–40 minutes or until well risen and firm to the touch.

4 Leave to cool in the tin for 10 minutes before turning out. Remove the lining paper and cool on a wire rack.

TOP TIP
To prevent the cake from over-browning, cover it with kitchen foil after 1 hour, if necessary.

STRAWBERRY CHEESECAKE

Serves 8
Preparation: about 15 minutes
Cooking time: about 50 minutes,
plus cooling
Freezing: not suitable
244 cals per slice

50g (2oz) margarine

75g (3oz) plain flour

25g (1oz) porridge oats

75g (3oz) caster sugar

2 x 340g (12oz) cartons natural
cottage cheese

2 eggs

60ml (4 tbsp) natural yogurt

225g (8oz) fresh strawberries

1 Grease and base-line a 20cm (8 inch) loose-bottomed round cake tin. Put the fat in a saucepan and heat until melted, then stir in the flour, oats and 25g (1oz) of the sugar. Stir together until well mixed, then press the mixture into the base of the cake tin. Bake in the oven at 180°C/350°F/ gas 4 for 10 minutes.

2 Meanwhile, rub the cottage cheese through a sieve into a bowl. Beat the eggs, then beat into the cottage cheese. Add the lemon rind and the remaining 50g (2oz) caster sugar and mix well together.

3 Pour the mixture into the cake tin. Return to the oven and bake for 20 minutes. Spoon the yogurt over the cheesecake and bake for a further 20 minutes. Leave to cool in the tin for 3–4 hours.

4 When cold, carefully remove the cheesecake from the tin. Hull and slice most of the strawberries and arrange, with the remaining whole berries, on top of the cheesecake before serving.

TOP TIP
Baking cheesecakes in spring-release tins makes turning out easy. If you do not have a spring-release tin, a cake tin with a loose base works almost as well.

BEST SMALL CAKES

GREEK EASTER CAKES

Makes 8
Preparation: 25 minutes, plus standing
Cooking time: 15–20 minutes
Freezing: not suitable
430 cals per cake

125g (4oz) unsalted butter, softened
100g (3½oz) caster sugar
finely grated rind of 1 lemon
60ml (4 tbsp) lemon juice
2 eggs
125g (4oz) semolina
10ml (2 tsp) baking powder
100g (3½oz) ground almonds

SYRUP
10 cardamom pods
1 orange
300g (10oz) caster sugar
200ml (7fl oz) water
juice of ½ lemon
1 cinnamon stick, halved
5ml (1 tsp) whole cloves
30ml (2 tbsp) orange flower water

1 Grease eight 150ml (¼ pint) dariole moulds.

2 Cream the butter and sugar together in a bowl until pale and fluffy. Beat in the lemon rind and juice, eggs, semolina, baking powder and ground almonds until the mixture is smooth.

3 Divide between the prepared moulds, level the surfaces and stand on a baking sheet. Bake at 200°C/400°F/gas 6 for about 15 minutes until just firm. Leave in the tins for 5 minutes then loosen with a knife, turn out and stand on a small tray.

4 For the syrup, lightly bruise the cardamom pods using a pestle and mortar or rolling pin. Pare thin strips of rind from the orange, then cut into fine shreds. Squeeze the juice.

5 Put the sugar and water in a small, heavy-based saucepan and heat gently until the sugar dissolves. Add the lemon juice, bring to the boil and boil rapidly for 3 minutes until syrupy. Stir in the orange shreds, orange juice, cardamom, cinnamon and cloves and heat gently for 5 minutes. Remove from the heat and stir in the orange flower water.

6 Spoon the syrup over the cakes, so each one becomes evenly steeped in syrup and the excess flows into the tray. Leave to cool, then chill until ready to serve. Serve the cakes with some of the strained syrup spooned over. Accompany with Greek yogurt or lightly whipped cream.

TOP TIP
If you haven't any dariole moulds, use six individual pudding moulds to make slightly larger cakes.

APRICOT PATTIES

Makes 12
Preparation: 15 minutes
Cooking time: 15–20 minutes
Freezing: suitable
270 cals per cake

410g (14½oz) can apricot halves in natural juice

175g (6oz) unsalted butter

175g (6oz) ground almonds

175g (6oz) caster sugar

75g (3oz) self-raising white flour, sifted

4 egg whites

icing sugar, for dusting

1 Lightly grease a non-stick 12-hole muffin or deep bun tin tray. Drain the apricots and leave to dry on kitchen paper. Melt the butter and leave to cool slightly.

2 Mix the ground almonds, sugar and flour together in a bowl. Add the egg whites and melted butter and stir until evenly mixed. Divide the mixture evenly between the sections and place an apricot half on each.

3 Bake at 200°C/400°F/gas 6 for 15–20 minutes until risen and golden. Leave in the tray for about 10 minutes to firm up slightly, then run a knife around the edges of the patties to loosen them. Transfer to a wire rack to cool. Serve dusted with icing sugar.

> **TOP TIP**
> If your muffin tray isn't non-stick, line with paper cases or baking parchment.

CHOCOLATE FILIGREE CAKES

Makes 16
Preparation: 30 minutes, plus cooling
Cooking time: 12–15 minutes
Freezing: suitable
210 cals per cake

2 eggs
50g (2oz) caster sugar
25g (1oz) plain white flour
25g (1oz) cocoa powder

FILLING
5ml (1 tsp) powdered gelatine
100ml (3½fl oz) milk
200g (7oz) white chocolate
1 egg
25g (1oz) caster sugar
5ml (1 tsp) vanilla essence
250g (9oz) mascarpone cheese
200g (7oz) Greek yogurt

TO DECORATE
25g (1oz) plain chocolate

1 Preheat the oven to 190°C/375°F/gas 5. Grease and base-line an 18cm (7 inch) square loose-bottomed cake tin.

2 Put the eggs and sugar in a large heatproof bowl over a pan of hot water and whisk until the mixture has doubled in volume and is thick enough to leave a trail on the surface when the whisk is lifted. Remove the bowl from the pan; whisk until cool.

3 Sift the flour and cocoa powder over the mixture, then fold in using a large metal spoon. Turn into the prepared tin and bake for 12–15 minutes until just firm to the touch. Turn out and cool on a wire rack.

4 Line the sides of the tin with fresh greaseproof paper. Slice the sponge in half horizontally and place one layer in the tin.

5 For the filling, sprinkle the gelatine over the milk in a small heatproof bowl and leave for 2–3 minutes. Break up the white chocolate and melt in a heatproof bowl set over a pan of simmering water.

6 Whisk together the egg, sugar and vanilla essence in a bowl until foamy. Place the bowl containing the softened gelatine over a pan of simmering water until the gelatine dissolves. Cool slightly, then pour over the white chocolate, stirring until smooth. Whisk into the egg mixture. Add the mascarpone and beat until smooth. Fold in the yogurt.

7 Spoon half the mixture over the sponge in the tin, then cover with the second sponge layer. Top with the remaining cheesecake mixture. Tap the tin gently to level the surface.

8 Melt the plain chocolate, put into a piping bag and pipe lines all over the surface of the cake. Chill until required. Carefully remove from the tin and peel away the paper. Use a sharp knife to cut the cake into 16 squares.

TOP TIP
If the cheesecake mixture becomes firm before you've layered the cake, beat in a little boiling water. If it's too thin, leave it to firm up a little before layering.

CRANBERRY MUFFINS

Makes 12
Preparation: 15 minutes
Cooking time: 15–18 minutes
Freezing: suitable
190 cals per muffin

125g (4oz) fresh or frozen
cranberries (see Top Tip)
25g (1oz) icing sugar, sifted
300g (10oz) plain white flour
10ml (2 tsp) baking powder
150g (5oz) light muscovado sugar
grated rind of 1 large orange
1 egg
5ml (1 tsp) vanilla essence
250ml (8fl oz) milk
50g (2oz) unsalted butter, melted
icing sugar, for dusting

1 Line a 12-hole muffin or deep bun tin tray with paper muffin cases (or simply grease if using a non-stick tray). Toss the cranberries in the icing sugar to coat.

2 Sift the flour and baking powder together into a bowl. Stir in the sugar, orange rind and cranberries.

3 In another bowl, beat together the egg, vanilla essence, milk and butter. Add to the dry ingredients and stir until the ingredients are just mixed together; do not over-mix.

4 Spoon into the prepared muffin tins and bake at 200°C/400°F/gas 6 for 15–18 minutes until risen or just firm. Transfer to a wire rack to cool. Serve warm or cold, dusted with icing sugar.

TOP TIP
If using frozen cranberries, thaw and dry them thoroughly on kitchen paper before tossing in the icing sugar.

ESPRESSO CAKES

Makes 7
Preparation: 30 minutes, plus cooling
Cooking time: 10–12 minutes
Freezing: suitable (stage 3)
280 cals per cake

3 eggs

75g (3oz) light or dark muscovado sugar

75g (3oz) plain white flour

MOCHA CUSTARD
15g (½oz) chocolate-coated coffee beans

40g (1½oz) caster sugar

20g (¾oz) cornflour

2 egg yolks

2.5ml (½ tsp) vanilla essence

200ml (7fl oz) milk

90ml (3fl oz) double cream

30ml (2 tbsp) finely ground espresso coffee

TO ASSEMBLE
cocoa powder, for dusting

90ml (3fl oz) double cream

10ml (2 tsp) finely ground espresso coffee

chopped chocolate-coated coffee beans, to decorate

1 Preheat the oven to 200°C/400°F/gas 6. Grease and line a 33 x 23cm (13 x 9 inch) Swiss roll tin.

2 Put the eggs and sugar in a large heatproof bowl over a pan of simmering water and whisk until the mixture is thick enough to leave a trail on the surface when the whisk is lifted. Remove the bowl from the pan and whisk until cooled.

3 Sift the flour over the whisked mixture and fold in carefully, using a large metal spoon. Turn into the prepared tin, gently easing the mixture into the corners. Bake for 10–12 minutes until well risen and just firm. Turn out onto a clean sheet of greaseproof paper and peel away the lining paper.

4 To make the custard, finely chop the chocolate-coated coffee beans. Place the sugar, cornflour, egg yolks, vanilla essence and a little of the milk in a bowl and beat until smooth. Put the rest of the milk, the cream and coffee in a saucepan and bring to the boil. Pour over the custard, stirring until smooth. Return to the heat and cook, stirring, for 2–3 minutes until thickened. Transfer to a bowl and cover the surface with a piece of greaseproof paper to prevent a skin forming. Leave to cool.

5 Using a 6cm (2½ inch) metal cutter, cut out 14 rounds from the sponge.

6 Spoon a little custard onto half of the rounds, then top with the remaining sponges. Dust generously with cocoa powder. Whip the cream until just peaking and spoon a little on top of each cake. Sprinkle with the ground espresso and decorate each cake with chopped chocolate-coated coffee beans. Chill until ready to serve.

TOP TIP
Espresso coffee gives a strong flavour. Use a milder coffee if preferred.

HONEY AND YOGURT MUFFINS

Makes 12
Preparation: 15 minutes
Cooking time: 17–20 minutes
Freezing: suitable
180 cals per muffin

225g (8oz) plain white flour
7.5ml (1½ tsp) baking powder
5ml (1 tsp) bicarbonate of soda
pinch of salt
2.5ml (½ tsp) ground mixed spice
1.25ml (¼ tsp) ground nutmeg
50g (2oz) medium oatmeal
50g (2oz) light muscovado sugar
50g (2oz) butter
225g (8oz) Greek yogurt
125ml (4fl oz) milk
1 egg
60ml (4 tbsp) clear honey
medium oatmeal, for dusting

1 Preheat the oven to 200°C/400°F/gas 6. Line a 12-hole muffin or deep bun tin tray with paper muffin cases. Sift the flour, baking powder, bicarbonate of soda, salt, mixed spice and nutmeg into a bowl. Stir in the oatmeal and sugar.

2 Melt the butter and leave to cool slightly. Mix the yogurt and milk together in a bowl, then beat in the egg, butter and honey.

3 Pour over the dry ingredients and stir in quickly until only just blended; do not over-mix.

4 Divide the mixture equally between the paper cases. Sprinkle with oatmeal and bake for 17–20 minutes until well risen and just firm to the touch. Remove from the oven and leave in the tins for 5 minutes, then transfer to a wire rack. Serve warm or cold, with a little butter if desired.

VARIATION
To make Chocolate Banana Muffins, omit the honey. Mash 1 small ripe banana and mix with 125g (4oz) melted plain chocolate. Add to the muffin mixture after the liquids, blending until rippled with colour.

HINNY CAKES

Makes 10
Preparation: 10 minutes
Cooking time: 14–18 minutes
Freezing: not suitable
190 cals per cake

175g (6oz) self-raising white flour
pinch of salt
5ml (1 tsp) baking powder
1.25ml (¼ tsp) ground mace
1.25ml (¼ tsp) ground cloves
75g (3oz) unsalted butter
25g (1oz) ground rice
25g (1 oz) caster sugar
90ml (3fl oz) milk
30ml (2 tbsp) sunflower oil

TO FINISH
225–350g (8–12oz) blueberries
40g (1½oz) caster sugar
lightly whipped cream, to serve

1 Sift the flour, salt, baking powder, mace and cloves into a bowl. Add 50g (2oz) of the butter, cut into small pieces, and rub in using your fingertips until the mixture resembles fine breadcrumbs. Stir in the ground rice and caster sugar. Add the milk and mix to a fairly soft dough, using a round-bladed knife.

2 Turn the dough out onto a lightly floured surface and knead very lightly. Cut into 10 even-sized pieces. Using lightly floured hands, shape each piece into a small flat cake.

3 Melt 15g (½oz) of the remaining butter with half the oil in a large heavy-based frying pan or griddle. Place half of the cakes in the pan and fry gently for 3–4 minutes until golden underneath. Turn the cakes over and cook for a further 3–4 minutes until cooked through. Transfer to a large baking sheet. Melt the remaining butter with the oil and fry the rest of the cakes.

4 Preheat the grill to medium. Spoon the blueberries onto the cakes, piling them up slightly in the centre. Sprinkle with the sugar. Place under the grill for about 2 minutes, watching closely, until the blueberries are bubbling and the cake edges are lightly toasted. Serve immediately, with whipped cream.

TOP TIP
It is essential to cook the cakes over a very gentle heat. A high temperature will overcook the crusts while the centres remain raw.

VARIATIONS
Use cranberries, or a mixture of dessert apples and blackberries instead of the blueberries. Serve with mascarpone cheese or Greek yogurt rather than whipped cream

CITRUS ECCLES CAKES

Makes 20
Preparation: 35 minutes, plus chilling
Cooking time: 12–15 minutes
Freezing: suitable
160 cals per cake

PASTRY
175g (6oz) firm unsalted butter
225g (8oz) plain white flour
pinch of salt
5ml (1 tsp) lemon juice

FILLING
175g (6oz) currants
50g (2oz) chopped mixed peel
50g (2oz) muscovado sugar
finely grated rind of 2 lemons

TO FINISH
beaten egg, to glaze
caster sugar, for dusting
50g (2oz) unsalted butter

1 To make the pastry, cut the butter into small dice. Sift the flour and salt into a bowl. Add the butter, lemon juice and 100ml (3½fl oz) iced water. Using a round-bladed knife mix to a soft dough, adding a little extra water if it is too dry.

2 Knead lightly, then roll out on a lightly floured surface to an oblong, about 30cm (12 inches) long and 10cm (4 inches) wide. Fold the bottom third up and the lower third down, keeping the edges straight, then give the pastry a quarter turn. Repeat the rolling, folding and turning four more times. Wrap in greaseproof paper and leave to rest in the refrigerator for 30 minutes.

3 For the filling, mix the currants, mixed peel, sugar and lemon rind together in a small bowl.

4 Preheat the oven to 220°C/425°F/gas 7. Lightly grease two baking sheets. Roll out half of the pastry on a lightly floured work surface to a 50 x 20cm (20 x 8 inch) rectangle. Cut in half lengthways, then cut each strip into five equal pieces.

5 Using the tip of a knife make three 2cm (¾ inch) cuts, 5mm (¼ inch) apart down the centre of one piece of pastry. Make three more rows of cuts either side of the first row so that when the pastry is pulled apart slightly it creates a lattice. Repeat with the remaining pieces of pastry. Brush the edges with beaten egg.

6 Set aside half of the filling. Divide the remainder between the latticed pastries, placing it in the centres. Bring the edges of the pastry up over the filling, pinching them together to seal. Invert onto one baking sheet, so the latticed sides face upwards.

7 Repeat with the remaining pastry and filling to make ten more pastries. Brush the pastries with beaten egg and sprinkle lightly with sugar. Bake for 12–15 minutes, until golden. Melt the butter and pour a little into each Eccles cake, through the lattice. Serve warm.

VARIATION
To make Cherry and Almond Cakes, replace the currants, peel and lemon rind with 125g (4oz) chopped glacé cherries, 50g (2oz) chopped blanched almonds and 125g (4oz) grated almond paste.

FIG AND OATMEAL MUFFINS

Makes 12
Preparation: 15 minutes
Cooking time: 15 minutes
Freezing: suitable
210 cals per muffin

225g (8oz) self-raising white flour
15ml (1 tbsp) baking powder
75g (3oz) medium oatmeal
175g (6oz) dried figs, chopped
125g (4oz) sultanas
75g (3oz) light muscovado sugar
75g (3oz) unsalted butter, melted
1 egg
finely grated rind of ½ orange
150ml (¼ pint) milk
extra oatmeal, for dusting

1 Line a 12-hole muffin or deep bun tin tray with paper muffin cases. Sift the flour and baking powder into a bowl. Stir in the oatmeal, figs, sultanas and sugar.

2 Mix together the butter, egg, orange rind and milk and pour into the bowl. Using a large metal spoon, fold the ingredients together lightly until just mixed.

3 Pile the mixture equally into the paper cases. Sprinkle with a little extra oatmeal and bake at 200°C/400°F/gas 6 for about 15 minutes until well risen and just firm to the touch. Transfer to a wire rack to cool. Serve warm.

TOP TIP
If you don't have a muffin tray and paper cases, make 'mini' muffins using ordinary paper cases in a sectioned tartlet tray, reducing the cooking time by a few minutes.

PEAR AND CINNAMON BUNS

Makes 14
Preparation: 10 minutes, plus cooling
Cooking time: about 15 minutes
Freezing: suitable (stage 2)
215 cals per bun

225g (8oz) self-raising white flour

2.5ml (½ tsp) ground cinnamon

125g (4oz) unsalted butter, in pieces

75g (3oz) caster sugar

125g (4oz) dried pears, roughly chopped

150g (5oz) sultanas

1 egg

90ml (3fl oz) milk

finely grated rind of 1 lemon

TO GLAZE
juice of 1 lemon

50g (2oz) caster sugar

15ml (1 tbsp) preserving sugar or crushed sugar cubes

1 Sift the flour and cinnamon together into a bowl. Rub in the butter, using your fingertips, until the mixture resembles fine breadcrumbs. Add the sugar, pears, sultanas, egg, milk and lemon rind; mix to a soft dough.

2 Spoon into about 14 small mounds on a greased large baking sheet. Bake at 190°C/375°F/gas 5 for about 15 minutes until risen and golden.

3 Meanwhile, make the glaze. Heat the lemon juice in a small, heavy-based saucepan with the sugar and 30ml (2 tbsp) water until the sugar has dissolved. Bring to the boil and boil for 3 minutes until syrupy.

4 On removing the buns from the oven, spoon on the glaze and sprinkle with the preserving sugar or crushed sugar cubes. Transfer to a wire rack to cool. These buns are best eaten with 1–2 days.

TOP TIP
If frozen, apply the glaze after the buns have thawed.

VARIATION
Use a mixture of dried peaches and apricots instead of the pears.

ALMOND FLOWER CAKES

Makes 15
Preparation: about 20 minutes
Cooking time: 20 minutes
Freezing: not suitable
156 cals per cake

175g (6oz) ground almonds

175g (6oz) caster sugar

15ml (1 tbsp) cornflour

2 egg whites

2–3 drops almond essence

about 75g (3oz) split blanched almonds (you need 75 almond pieces in total)

small pieces of red or green glacé cherry

1 Very lightly grease the base and sides of a 28 x 18cm (11 x 7 inch) shallow oblong tin and line with a sheet of non-stick baking parchment.

2 In a bowl, mix the ground almonds with the sugar, cornflour, unbeaten egg whites and almond essence, working the ingredients together until well blended.

3 Transfer the mixture to the tin and spread out level. Lightly mark into 15 pieces (but do not cut right through) and arrange 5 split almonds and a small piece of glacé cherry in the centre of each one to form a flower design.

4 Bake at 180°C/350°F/gas 4 for 15 minutes until golden, then cover with foil and continue for a further 5 minutes.

5 Carefully cut the almond mixture into 15 pieces while still hot and run a knife around the sides of the tin to prevent the mixture sticking. Leave to cool in the tin.

BEST TRAYBAKES AND TEABREADS

APPLE, SULTANA AND CIDER SLICES

Makes 12 slices
Preparation: 25 minutes
Cooking time: 1 hour
Freezing: suitable (without glaze)
380 cals per slice

225g (8oz) puff pastry

3 dessert apples

15ml (1 tbsp) lemon juice

175g (6oz) unsalted butter, softened

175g (6oz) caster sugar

125g (4oz) self-raising white flour

75g (3oz) self-raising wholemeal flour

2.5ml (½ tsp) baking powder

3 eggs

45ml (3 tbsp) medium dry cider

50g (2oz) sultanas

10ml (2 tsp) icing sugar

TO FINISH
icing sugar, for sprinkling

1 Preheat the oven to 200°C/400°F/gas 6. Lightly dampen a large baking sheet. Roll out the pastry thinly on a lightly floured surface to a 28cm (11 inch) square and place on a baking sheet. Prick all over with a fork and bake for 10 minutes until risen. Reduce the oven temperature to 180°C/350°F/gas 4.

2 Lightly grease a 23cm (9 inch) square shallow baking tin. Cut the pastry to fit the base of the tin, then carefully press into position.

3 Peel, core and slice one of the apples. Place in a bowl of water with 5ml (1 tsp) of the lemon juice. Core and slice the remaining apples and place in a separate bowl with the remaining lemon juice.

4 Cream the butter and sugar together in a bowl until pale and creamy. Sift the flours and baking powder into a bowl. Add the eggs and cider and beat well until smooth. Drain the peeled apple slices and stir into the mixture with the sultanas. Spoon over the pastry and level the surface.

5 Drain the unpeeled apple slices and arrange over the filling. Dust with the icing sugar and bake for 45–50 minutes until just firm. Leave to cool in the tin for 15 minutes.

6 Dust with icing sugar and serve warm, cut into squares.

TOP TIP
If you don't have a suitable square tin, use a 23cm (9 inch) loose-based round cake tin instead.

VARIATION
Instead of dusting with icing sugar, apply a cider-flavoured glaze. Sift 125g (4oz) icing sugar into a bowl and stir in 30ml (2 tbsp) cider to make a smooth icing. Pour over the warm cake, leaving some of the apple slices exposed.

SESAME PRUNE SLICES

Makes 16 slices
Preparation: 20 minutes, plus cooling
Cooking time: 35 minutes
Freezing: suitable
295 cals per slice

BASE
175g (6oz) plain white flour
125g (4oz) unsalted butter or margarine
50g (2oz) caster sugar

FILLING
225g (8oz) no-need-to-soak dried prunes
15g (½oz) dark muscovado sugar
2.5ml (½ tsp) cornflour

TOPPING
125g (4oz) unsalted butter or margarine
75g (3oz) caster sugar
15ml (1 tbsp) honey
125g (4oz) no-need-to-soak dried prunes
125g (4oz) self-raising white flour
2.5ml (½ tsp) bicarbonate of soda
125g (4oz) medium oatmeal
50g (2oz) sesame seeds

1 Preheat the oven to 180°C/350°F/gas 4. Grease a baking tin measuring 22 x 29cm (8½ x 11½ inches) across the top and 19 x 27cm (7½ x 10½ inches) across the base. (Or use a tin with similar dimensions.)

2 To make the base, sift the flour into a bowl. Add the butter or margarine, cut into small pieces, and rub in using your fingertips. Stir in the sugar until the mixture begins to cling together.

3 Turn into the tin and pack the mixture down well with the back of a spoon. Bake for 15 minutes until turning golden around the edges.

4 For the filling, roughly chop the prunes and place in a small saucepan with the sugar and 150ml (¼ pint) water. Bring to the boil, reduce the heat, cover and simmer gently for 10 minutes. Blend the cornflour with 15ml (1 tbsp) water and add to the pan. Cook for 1 minute, stirring until the juices have thickened. Leave to cool slightly, then spread over the shortbread base.

5 For the topping, place the butter or margarine, sugar and honey in a small pan and heat gently until dissolved. Finely chop the prunes and stir into the mixture.

6 Sift the flour and bicarbonate of soda into a bowl. Add the oatmeal and all but 30ml (2 tbsp) of the sesame seeds. Add the melted mixture and beat until evenly combined.

7 Spoon the topping over the prunes in the tin and level the surface. Bake for 20 minutes or until the topping is golden and slightly risen. Leave to cool in the tin, then cut into bars. Store in an airtight tin for up to 5 days.

TOP TIP
A food processor is ideal for mixing the base, and for finely chopping the prunes before adding to the topping.

VARIATIONS
Use other plump dried fruit such as apricots, figs or dates instead of prunes.
Add a pinch of mixed spice or grated lemon rind to the topping.

SYROPY SEMOLINA HALVA

Makes 10 slices
Preparation: 30 minutes
Cooking time: 30 minutes
Freezing: suitable (stage 2)
485 cals per slice

125g (4oz) unsalted butter,
softened

125g (4oz) light muscovado sugar

grated rind of 1 orange

grated rind of 1 lemon

30ml (2 tbsp) lemon juice

2 eggs

175g (6oz) semolina

5ml (1 tsp) baking powder

125g (4oz) ground almonds

30ml (2 tbsp) poppy seeds

TO FINISH
2 oranges

2 lemons

300g (10oz) caster sugar

300ml (½ pint) freshly squeezed
orange juice

2 cinnamon sticks, halved

1 Preheat the oven to 220°C/425°F/gas 7. Grease and base-line a shallow 23cm (9 inch) square baking tin. Cream the butter and sugar together until pale and fluffy.

2 Add the orange and lemon rind, lemon juice, eggs, semolina, baking powder, ground almonds and poppy seeds. Beat well until evenly mixed, then turn into the prepared tin and level the surface. Bake for about 20 minutes until slightly risen and turning golden. Remove from the oven and leave to cool in the tin. Peel off the paper, then return to the tin.

3 To finish, finely pare the rind from 1 orange and 1 lemon in strips using a citrus zester. Cut away the white pith from both oranges and lemons, then thinly slice the fruit. Place the sugar in a heavy-based saucepan with the orange juice, cinnamon sticks and pared fruit rind. Heat gently, stirring until the sugar dissolves, then bring to the boil and boil for 3 minutes.

4 Remove the pared fruit rind and cinnamon from the syrup with a slotted spoon and reserve. Pour just over half of the syrup evenly over the surface of the cake. Scatter the fruit slices, pared rind and cinnamon sticks on top.

5 Return the remaining syrup to the heat and cook for another 5 minutes or until thickened and beginning to caramelise. Pour over the fruit and leave for several hours before cutting. Store in an airtight plastic container for up to 4–5 days.

TOP TIP
If preferred, arrange the decorative fruits in line to make cutting easier.

STICKY ORANGE FLAPJACKS

Makes 18
Preparation: 10 minutes
Cooking time: 25–30 minutes
Freezing: suitable
300 cals per flapjack

2 small oranges

250g (9oz) unsalted butter

250g (9oz) caster sugar

175g (6oz) golden syrup

425g (15oz) porridge oats

30ml (2 tbsp) sunflower seeds

45ml (3 tbsp) fine-shred orange marmalade

1 Preheat the oven to 180°C/350°F/gas 4. Grease a baking tin measuring 22 x 29cm (8½ x 11½ inches) across the top and 19 x 27cm (7½ x 10½ inches) across the base. (Or use a tin with similar dimensions.)

2 Using a citrus zester, finely pare the rind from the oranges in strips. Place in a heavy-based saucepan. Add the butter, cut into pieces, with the sugar and syrup. Cook over a moderate heat, stirring until the butter has melted. Remove from the heat and stir in the oats, until evenly coated in syrup.

3 Turn the mixture into the prepared tin and level the surface. Sprinkle with the sunflower seeds. Bake for 25–30 minutes until turning deep golden around the edges; the mixture will still be very soft in the centre. Leave in the tin until almost cold.

4 Heat the marmalade in a small saucepan with 15ml (1 tbsp) water until syrupy. Brush evenly over the flapjack. Turn out onto a board and cut into 18 bars. Store in an airtight container for up to 1 week.

TOP TIP
To weigh syrup, first measure out the sugar quantity and leave it in the scales bowl, making a small well in the centre. Add additional weights for the required quantity of syrup and spoon the syrup into the well. Both sugar and syrup will then slide cleanly into the saucepan.

WHITE CHOCOLATE BROWNIES

Makes 12
Preparation: 20 minutes
Cooking time: 30–35 minutes
Freezing: suitable
490 cals per brownie

175g (6oz) shelled hazelnuts
500g (1lb 2oz) white chocolate
75g (3oz) butter
3 eggs
175g (6oz) caster sugar
175g (6oz) self-raising white flour
pinch of salt
5ml (1 tsp) vanilla essence

1 Preheat the oven to 190°C/375°F/gas 5. Grease and line a baking tin measuring 22 x 29cm (8½ x 11½ inches) across the top and 19 x 27cm (7½ x 10½ inches) across the base. (Or use a tin with similar dimensions.)

2 Roughly chop the hazelnuts. Roughly chop 400g (14oz) of the chocolate and set aside. Break up the remaining chocolate and put into a heatproof bowl with the butter. Place over a pan of simmering water until melted. Leave to cool slightly.

3 Whisk the eggs and sugar together in a large bowl until smooth, then gradually beat in the melted chocolate mixture. Sift the flour and salt over the mixture, then fold in with the hazelnuts, chopped chocolate and vanilla essence.

4 Turn the mixture into the prepared tin and level the surface. Bake for 30–35 minutes until risen and golden, and the centre is just firm to the touch. Leave to cool in the tin. Turn out and cut into 12 squares. Store in an airtight container for up to 1 week.

TOP TIP
When cooked, the mixture will still be very soft under the crust; it firms up during cooling.

VARIATIONS
Use any other roughly chopped nuts instead of the hazelnuts. Almond, walnuts, pecans and brazil nuts are suitable.

APPLE AND BLACKBERRY SCONE

Makes 6 slices
Preparation: 15 minutes
Cooking time: 50 minutes
Freezing: suitable
300 cals per slice

1 cooking apple, about 175g (6oz)

25g (1oz) caster sugar

8 cloves

75g (3oz) blackberries

10ml (2 tsp) cornflour

200g (7oz) self-raising white flour

pinch of salt

2.5ml ($\frac{1}{2}$ tsp) ground cinnamon

5ml (1 tsp) baking powder

75g (3oz) unsalted butter

25g (1oz) medium oatmeal

50g (2oz) light muscovado sugar

90ml (3fl oz) milk

TO FINISH
milk, to glaze

demerara sugar and medium oatmeal, for sprinkling

75g (3oz) blackberries

1 Preheat the oven to 200°C/400°F/gas 6. Lightly grease a 19–20cm (7½–8 inch) spring-release cake tin. Peel, core and thinly slice the apple. Place in a bowl with the sugar, cloves, blackberries and cornflour; toss gently to mix.

2 Sift the flour, salt, cinnamon and baking powder together and place in a food processor. Add the butter, cut into small pieces, and work until the mixture resembles breadcrumbs. Add the oatmeal and sugar. Add most of the milk and process briefly to a soft dough, adding the remaining milk if the mixture is too dry.

3 On a floured surface, roll out two-thirds of the dough to a round about 23cm (9 inches) in diameter. Use to line the tin, so that the dough comes about 2.5cm (1 inch) up the sides. Pile the apple and blackberry mixture into the centre and brush the edges with a little milk.

4 Roll out the remaining dough to a 19–20cm (7½–8 inch) round and lay over the filling, pressing the edges gently together to secure.

5 Brush with milk and mark into 6 wedges. Sprinkle with the demerara sugar and oatmeal and bake for 30 minutes until well risen and golden. Reduce the oven temperature to 160°C/325°F/gas 3.

6 Scatter the scone with the remaining blackberries and sprinkle with more sugar and oatmeal. Return to the oven for a further 20 minutes, covering with foil if the scone appears to be turning too brown. Leave in the tin for 5 minutes, then transfer to a wire rack to cool.

VARIATIONS
Use pears (preferably the cooking variety) in place of apple. Alternatively, use peaches and substitute raspberries for the blackberries.

FRUITED HONEY TEABREAD

Makes 10 slices
Preparation: 10 minutes, plus
overnight soaking
Cooking time: 1–1¼ hours
Freezing: suitable
320 cals per slice

50g (2oz) ready-to-eat apricots,
roughly chopped

50g (2oz) ready-to-eat prunes,
roughly chopped

225g (8oz) raisins

150g (5oz) dark muscovado sugar

300ml (½ pint) strong tea, strained

125g (4oz) plain wholemeal flour

125g (4oz) self-raising white flour

5ml (1 tsp) baking powder

5ml (1 tsp) ground cinnamon

75g (3oz) brazil nuts, roughly
chopped

2 eggs

125g (4oz) clear honey

extra honey, warmed, to glaze
(optional)

1 Mix the apricots, prunes, raisins and sugar together in a bowl. Pour on the tea, cover and leave to soak overnight.

2 Grease and line a 1.2 litre (2 pint) loaf tin. Sift the flours, baking powder and cinnamon into a bowl. Add the soaked fruits and liquid, brazil nuts, eggs and honey. Mix until evenly combined.

3 Turn into the prepared loaf tin and bake at 180°C/350°F/gas 4 for 1–1¼ hours, or until firm and a skewer inserted into the centre comes out clean.

4 Leave to cool in the tin. Drizzle with a little extra honey to glaze if liked.

VARIATION
Use roughly chopped walnuts instead of brazil nuts.

APPLE AND GINGER TEABREAD

Makes 8 slices
Preparation: 20 minutes, plus cooling
Cooking time: 1–1¼ hours
Freezing: suitable
410 cals per slice

4 crisp, tart dessert apples, such as Granny Smith's

15ml (1 tbsp) lemon juice

125g (4oz) unsalted butter

75g (3oz) light muscovado sugar

200g (7oz) golden syrup

300g (10oz) self-raising white flour

2.5ml (½ tsp) baking powder

2.5ml (½ tsp) ground cinnamon

2.5ml (½ tsp) ground cloves

1 egg

75g (3oz) preserved stem ginger in syrup, drained and finely chopped

45ml (3 tbsp) golden syrup, warmed, to serve (optional)

1 Grease and line a 1.2 litre (2 pint) loaf tin. Peel, core and thinly slice the apples; immerse in a bowl of cold water with the lemon juice added.

2 Put the butter, sugar and syrup in a saucepan and heat until melted; cool slightly.

3 Sift the flour, baking powder and spices into a bowl. Add the syrup mixture and egg; stir until well combined.

4 Thoroughly drain the apple slices on kitchen paper. Add three-quarters of them and all but 15ml (1 tbsp) of the ginger to the cake mixture; stir until evenly combined.

5 Turn into the prepared loaf tin and scatter over the reserved apple slices and ginger. Bake at 170°C/325°F/gas 3 for 1–1¼ hours until just firm and a skewer inserted into the centre comes out clean.

6 Leave in the tin for 15 minutes, then spoon over the syrup. Allow to cool completely before slicing. Eat within 4–5 days.

FRUIT AND SPICE PARKIN

Makes 12 slices
Preparation: 10 minutes, plus cooling
Cooking time: 1¼–1½ hours
Freezing: suitable
440 cals per slice

225g (8oz) dried figs, thinly sliced

125g (4oz) sultanas

200ml (7fl oz) apple or orange juice

175g (6oz) black treacle

175g (6oz) golden syrup

125g (4oz) unsalted butter

250g (9oz) plain white flour

15ml (1 tbsp) ground mixed spice

10ml (2 tsp) baking powder

65g (2½oz) light muscovado sugar

250g (9oz) medium oatmeal

1 egg

1 Grease and line a 20cm (8 inch) square cake tin. Put the figs and sultanas in a saucepan with the fruit juice. Bring to the boil, then take off the heat and leave to cool.

2 Put the treacle, syrup and butter in a saucepan and heat until the butter is melted; cool slightly.

3 Sift the flour, spice and baking powder into a bowl. Stir in the sugar and oatmeal. Add half the dried fruits with any juices, the syrup mixture and egg; stir until well combined. Turn into the prepared tin and scatter over the reserved fruit.

4 Bake at 170°C/325°F/gas 3 for 1¼–1½ hours until just firm and a skewer inserted into the centre comes out clean. Leave to cool in the tin.

5 Once cold, wrap in greaseproof paper and store in an airtight container for 1–2 weeks to mature before eating.

VARIATION
Use chopped ready-to-eat prunes or dried dates instead of the figs.

APPLE AND ALMOND BAKE

Serves 6
Preparation: about 25 minutes
Cooking time: 20–25 minutes
Freezing: not suitable
603 cals per slice

175g (6oz) butter

1.1kg (2lb) crisp eating apples,
cored and cut into thick wedges

150g (5oz) caster sugar

finely grated rind and juice of
1 lemon

175g (6oz) ground almonds

3 eggs

single cream, to serve

1 Melt 50g (2oz) of the butter in a large frying pan until foaming. Add the apples, scatter 25g (1oz) of the sugar on top and cook briskly for about 5 minutes, turning the apple wedges once or twice until softened and beginning to brown.

2 Meanwhile, place all but 15ml (1 tbsp) of the remaining sugar in a mixing bowl. Add the remaining butter and beat until light and fluffy, then beat in the lemon rind and juice, almonds and eggs.

3 Transfer the apples to a well-buttered baking dish, then pour the almond mixture over. Tap the dish on the work surface once or twice to settle the mixture.

4 Bake in the oven at 200°C/400°F/gas 6 for 20–25 minutes, until the topping is set and golden brown. Sprinkle with the reserved sugar. Serve warm, with single cream.

BEST EASY NOVELTY CAKES

FLUFFY SHEEP

Madeira cake mixture made
with 125g (4oz) plain flour
(see page 12)

½ quantity butter cream
(see page 19)

25cm (10 inch) round cake board

250g (9oz) ready-to-roll icing

brown, green and black food
colourings

1 quantity royal icing
(see page 20)

1 Make the cake mixture, turn into a prepared 3.4 litre (6 pint) ovenproof bowl (see Top Tip) and bake for about 1¼ hours until just firm. Leave to cool in the bowl, then loosen the edges with a palette knife to ease the cake out of the bowl.

2 Cut off any dome from the top of the cake, then split the cake horizontally into three layers. Sandwich together with all but 30ml (2 tbsp) of the butter cream and place on the cake board. Spread with the remaining butter cream.

3 Colour 150g (5oz) of the ready-to-roll icing brown and the rest green, leaving a small ball of white. Roll out the green icing thinly and use to cover the cake board. Trim off the excess icing.

4 Spread the royal icing all over the cake in an even layer, then swirl lightly with the tip of a knife. Roll two-thirds of the brown icing into a ball and flatten into an oval shape. Press gently onto the top of the cake.

5 From the remaining brown icing, shape two small ears and two front feet; press into the icing. (If necessary, prop the ears on balls of crumpled foil until they set.)

6 Make two eyes in white icing and secure in position with a dampened paintbrush. Using black food colouring and a fine paintbrush, paint the features to complete the cake.

TOP TIP

To prepare an ovenproof bowl, first grease the bowl. Cut out a circle of greaseproof paper which covers the base and goes slightly up the sides. Make 2.5cm (1 inch) cuts from the edge of the circle towards the centre at 2.5cm (1 inch) intervals. Fit into the base and grease the paper.

ROBOT

Victoria sandwich cake mixture made with 175g (6oz) flour (see page 14)

½ quantity butter cream (see page 19)

jam, for filling (optional)

20cm (8 inch) round cake board (optional)

black and yellow food colourings

1 round biscuit (any type)

25g (1oz) ready-to-roll icing

1 tube of Smarties

1 packet of Jelly Tots

1 packet of fruit Polos

3 lollipops

1 Grease and base-line a 1.1 litre (2 pint) pudding basin, a 300ml (½ pint) pudding basin and a bun tin (or use a paper fairy cake case). Make the cake mixture and spoon into the prepared basins and bun tin. Bake in the oven at 190°C/375°F/gas 5. Bake the smaller cakes for 20–30 minutes and the large one for about 45–60 minutes. Turn out, remove the lining papers and leave to cool on a wire rack.

2 Slice the large cake in half and sandwich together with jam, if using, or some of the butter cream. Set the large cake on the cake board, if using, or on a serving plate. Attach the small cake to the top with a little butter cream. Colour the rest of the butter cream pale grey and use to cover the cake completely.

3 Attach the bun to the biscuit with butter cream, then spread butter cream on top of the bun. Colour the ready-to-roll icing yellow and roll out thinly. Use to cover the bun and biscuit.

4 Arrange rows of Smarties on the lower half of the cake and add two for the eyes. Arrange Jelly Tots around the join between the head and the base of the robot. Put the yellow covered bun on top. Thread three fruit Polos onto one of the lollipops and push into the top of the robot. Do the same with the other two lollipops and push into the cake at the front.

TOP TIP
Decorate the robot with the birthday child's favourite sweets.

PINK PIG

Madeira cake mixture made with 175g (6oz) plain flour (see page 12)

1 quantity butter cream (see page 19)

jam, for filling

1.25kg (2lb 12oz) ready-to-roll icing

red, pink and black food colourings

23cm (9 inch) round cake board

1 Grease and base-line two 600ml (1 pint) ovenproof bowls with greaseproof paper (see Top Tip on page 142). Make the cake mixture, turn into the bowls and level the surfaces. Bake for about 50 minutes or until just firm. Leave to cool in the bowls, then loosen the edges with a palette knife and ease the cakes out of the bowls.

2 Colour 150g (5oz) of the ready-to-roll icing red and the remainder pink.

3 Cut the domes off the top of the cakes. Halve each cake horizontally. Sandwich each cake with butter cream and jam, then sandwich the two cakes together with more butter cream and jam.

4 Dampen the cake board with water. Roll out the red icing and use to cover the board, trimming off the excess around the edges.

5 Roll out just under half of the pink icing to a 33cm (13 inch) round and lay it over the cake. Ease the icing around the sides, trimming to fit in an even layer. (Don't worry too much about the finish as the cake will have a second layer of icing.) Smooth the icing down with the palms of your hands and leave to set overnight in a cool place.

6 Transfer the cake to the cake board. Reserve 150g (5oz) of the remaining pink icing. Roll out the rest to a round as before and use to cover the cake in a second layer, this time trimming and smoothing out as many joins as possible.

7 Roll a little icing into a ball and flatten into a 'snout'. Secure to the front of the cake and make two nostrils using the end of a paintbrush. Shape four small balls of icing for the pig's feet and make a deep cut into each. Position on the cake.

8 Shape two large flat ears and a small curly tail and secure in place. Paint the eyes and mouth using black food colouring and a fine paintbrush.

SEA SCENE

Victoria sandwich cake mixture
made with 225g (8oz) flour
(see page 14)

1 quantity butter cream
(see page19)

jam, for filling

30cm (12 inch) round cake board

1.3kg (3lb) ready-to-roll icing

blue, orange, green, yellow and
red food colourings

birthday candles

1 Make the cake mixture and turn into two prepared 20cm (8 inch) round sandwich tins. Bake for about 30 minutes or until just firm to the touch. Turn out, remove the lining paper and leave to cool on a wire rack.

2 Sandwich the cakes with half the butter cream and the jam and place on the cake board. Spread with the remaining butter cream.

3 Colour 1kg (2lb 4oz) of the ready-to-roll icing blue, 125g (4oz) orange, 50g (2oz) green, 50g (2oz) yellow and 50g (2oz) red. Leave a tiny amount white for the eyes of the octopus and fish and for the water ripples on top of the cake.

4 Reserve 175g (6oz) of the blue icing. Roll out the remainder and use to cover the cake, smoothing it to fit around the sides. Trim off the excess icing around the base. Dampen the edges of the cake board. Roll out the remaining blue icing and use to cover the edges of the board. Trim off the excess.

5 Roll about half the orange icing into a ball and make it slightly pear shaped at one end. Cut off an angled slice from one thin end and secure to the top of the cake. Roll the remaining orange icing into eight long tentacles, thinning each to a point at one end. Position each tentacle on the cake, wrapping the appropriate number of candles at the ends.

6 Roll out the green icing thinly and cut out seaweed shapes. Secure at various intervals around the sides of the cake.

7 From the remaining colours, shape a selection of different fish and starfish and secure around the sides. With the white icing, add the eyes to the octopus and fish and put a few ripples on the surface of the cake. Use a fine paintbrush and diluted food colourings to paint the features onto the octopus' face.

RED BUS

Madeira cake mixture made with 175g (6oz) plain flour (see page 12)

1 quantity butter cream (see page 19)

jam, for filling

1kg (2lb 4oz) ready-to-roll icing

red, black, blue, yellow and silver food colourings

25cm (10 inch) round cake board

1 candy or chocolate stick

4 liquorice Catherine wheels

1 Make the cake mixture and turn into a prepared 18cm (7 inch) square cake tin. Bake for about 1½ hours or until the cake springs back when pressed gently in the centre.

2 Slice the dome off the top of the cake and halve the cake, first horizontally, then vertically. Stack the rectangles of cake on top of one another, sandwiching the layers with half the butter cream and the jam. Using a small knife, cut out a square from the front of the cake for the area next to the driver's cab and another at the back left-hand side of the cake for the platform.

3 Colour 650g (1lb 7oz) of the icing red, 200g (7oz) grey, 100g (3½oz) light blue, 15g (½oz) yellow and 15g (½oz) black, leaving the rest white. Lightly dampen the cake board. Roll out the grey icing thinly and use to cover the cake board, trimming off the excess. Place the cake on the board and spread with the remaining butter cream.

4 Roll out the red icing and use to cover the cake, one side at a time, finishing with the cut-out areas at the back and front. Once all the sections are covered, smooth out the icing with the palms of your hands.

5 Shape a small square of black icing and use to cover the base of the platform at the back. Trim the candy or chocolate stick to the right length and push into position.

6 Roll out the blue icing thinly and cut into rectangles. Secure around the cake for the windows. From the yellow and white icing, shape and position the radiator, bus number plate, route number plate, headlights and road markings.

7 Unroll the liquorice wheels until they're a suitable size for bus wheels. Secure to the sides with blobs of red icing trimmings.

8 Using a paintbrush and silver food colouring, paint the radiator and the edges of the headlights. Write the child's name on the bus number plate and age on the route number plate. Dilute a little black or blue food colouring and use to scribble faint lines over the windows.

HOT WHEELS

Madeira cake mixture made
with 175g (6oz) plain flour
(see page 12)

1 quantity butter cream
(see page 19)

jam, for filling

23cm (9 inch) square cake board

1kg (2lb 4oz) ready-to-roll icing

red, black, yellow, orange, yellow
and silver food colourings

1 Make the cake mixture and turn into a prepared 18cm (7 inch) square cake tin. Bake for 1½ hours until the cake springs back when pressed. Leave to cool in the tin, then turn out.

2 Cut the dome off the top of the cake. Halve the cake horizontally and sandwich with some butter cream and jam. Then halve the cake vertically and sandwich the two layers together so the cake block is about 10cm (4 inches) deep.

3 Cut out a wedge from one end of the cake for the bonnet area. Cut another wedge from under the bumper area at the front. Colour 450g (1lb) of the ready-to-roll icing red, 375g (13oz) black, 125g (4oz) grey (using a little black food colouring) and the remainder yellow.

4 Lightly dampen the cake board. Roll out the grey icing thinly and use to cover the board. Spread the remaining butter cream over the cake. Place on the board.

5 Roll out two-thirds of the red icing to a strip about 35 x 9cm (14 x 3½ inches). Lay over the cake, starting at the bottom edge of the back, then laying it over the roof and front of the cake, tucking it under at the front. Trim off any excess. Use the remaining red icing to cover the sides of the cake. Leave for several hours to harden.

6 Roll out the yellow icing thinly. Dampen the front corners of the cake and lay the yellow icing over to cover the flame area. Using a scalpel or fine-bladed knife, cut through the yellow icing to shape the flames, removing the excess icing. Shape more flames from the trimmings and secure onto the sides of the cake.

7 Thinly roll out some black icing and cut a long strip, about 2cm (¾ inch) wide. Secure all around the base of the cake. Shape and position black icing for the windows.

8 Shape a long thin strip of black icing for the bumper and secure to the front of the cake. Divide the remaining black icing into four and shape each into large wheels. Make tyre markings with a knife and secure the wheels to the sides of the cake.

9 Using a fine paintbrush and silver food colouring, paint the window edges, bumper and wheel centres.

FIRST TELEPHONE

Madeira cake mixture made with 125g (4oz) plain flour (see page 12)

½ quantity butter cream (see page 19)

jam, for filling

800g (1lb 12oz) ready-to-roll icing

yellow, blue and red food colourings

20cm (8 inch) square cake board

5 Smarties

1 Make the cake mixture and turn into a prepared 15cm (6 inch) square cake tin. Bake for about 1¼ hours, or until the cake is a deep golden colour and feels firm to the touch. Leave to cool in the tin, then turn out and leave on a wire rack to cool completely.

2 Cut a small sloping wedge from the cake, finishing about 2cm (¾ inch) down one side, then cut off 1cm (½ inch) from the two opposite sides. Halve the cake horizontally and sandwich with half the butter cream and the jam.

3 Colour 400g (14oz) of the ready-to-roll icing yellow, 125g (4oz) very light blue, 75g (3oz) dark blue and 200g (7oz) red, leaving a tiny ball of white for the eyes. Dampen the cake board with water. Roll out the light blue icing thinly and use to cover the board, trimming off the excess around the edges. Position the cake on the board and spread with the remaining butter cream.

4 Roll out the yellow icing and use to cover the cake. Smooth it to fit around the sides and trim off the excess around the base. Roll 150g (5oz) of the red icing into a thick sausage, 16cm (6¼ inches) long. Dampen the highest point of the yellow icing with water and position the red icing for the receiver, smoothing it down lightly.

5 Cut out a 9cm (3½ inch) circle from the remaining red icing, then press out small holes using a small cutter or wide end of a piping nozzle. Secure to the telephone and press a Smartie into the centre. Use the white icing to shape two eyes and position above the dial, adding blue centres and small eyebrows from the red trimmings.

6 Divide the remaining blue icing into four pieces and shape into wheels. Secure at the sides of the cake and press a Smartie into the centre of each. If you like, finish the cake by writing the child's name and age on the dial.

PAINTBOX

Victoria sandwich cake mixture
made with 175g (6oz) flour
(see page 14)

½ quantity butter cream
(see page 19)

35 x 25cm (14 x 10 inch)
rectangular board or tray

1kg (2lb 4oz) ready-to-roll icing

blue, yellow, pink, black, red and
green food colourings

1 Make the cake mixture, turn into a prepared 28 x 18cm (11 x 7 inch) rectangular shallow tin and bake for 25–30 minutes until just firm. Turn out, remove the lining paper and place on a wire rack to cool.

2 Colour 325g (11oz) of the ready-to-roll icing dark blue, 15g (½oz) light blue, 35g (1¼oz) yellow, 35g (1¼ oz) pink, 35g (1¼ oz) black, 15g (½oz) red, 15g (½oz) dark green and 15g (½oz) light green, leaving the remainder white.

3 Invert the cake so the base is uppermost and cut out a long, deep groove from the centre, almost to the ends of the sponge. Position on the board and spread with the butter cream.

4 Roll out three-quarters of the white icing the same size as the cake (use the tin as a guide) and position on the cake. Using a 5cm (2 inch) round cutter, cut out eight circles from the top of the cake. Use a twisting action so the icing doesn't become too displaced.

5 Roll out the dark blue icing and cut out long thin strips 3cm (1¼ inches) wide. Use to cover the sides of the cake.

6 Take 15g (½oz) balls of each of the coloured icings. Roll each into a neat ball shape and flatten to a 5cm (2 inch) round. Use to fill in the holes on top of the cake. Roll out the white icing thinly and cut out shapes to resemble paper. Arrange on the cake board, securing them with a dampened paintbrush and cutting them to fit around the box and edges of the board or tray.

7 Use the remaining coloured icings to shape two paintbrushes and place on the cake and board. Dilute two or three of the food colourings and paint lines (or a message if you prefer) on the white icing.

BIRD HOUSE

Madeira cake mixture made with 125g (4oz) plain flour (see page 12)

1 quantity butter cream (see page 19)

jam, for filling

1.1kg (2lb 8oz) ready-to-roll icing

green, brown, red, yellow, orange and blue food colourings

23cm (9 inch) round cake board

1 shredded wheat

1 Grease and base-line a 23cm (9 inch) cake tin. Make the cake mixture and turn into the prepared tin. Bake for about 1¼ hours, or until the cake is firm and a skewer inserted in the centre comes out clean. Leave to cool in the tin.

2 Cut off the dome from the top of the cake then cut the cake vertically into quarters. Use half the butter cream and all the jam to sandwich the cakes together into a stack.

3 Cut off two wedges from the top sponge to shape a roof. Press a 7.5cm (3 inch) cutter into one end of the house. Remove it and scoop out about 2.5cm (1 inch) depth of sponge.

4 Colour 125g (4oz) of the icing green, 500g (1lb 2oz) brown, 250g (9oz) red, 50g (2oz) yellow and 15g (½oz) orange, leaving the remainder white.

5 Dampen the cake board with water. Roll out the green icing thinly and use to cover the board, trimming off the excesss around the edges. Position the cake on the board and spread with the remaining butter cream.

6 Roll out the brown icing and use to cover the sides of the bird house, one side at a time. Mark the horizontal lines using the back of a knife. Use the brown icing trimmings to line the hole in the cake. Dampen the icing in the hole. Break up the shredded wheat and press it into the soft icing to secure.

7 For the roof, roll out the red icing to a 15 x 13cm (6 x 5 inch) rectangle. Position on top of the cake with the longer sides at the front and back of the cake. Smooth down gently.

8 Roll the yellow icing into three small balls for the birds' heads. Snip the tops with scissors. Cut out three orange diamond shapes and fold in half for the beaks. Press into position. Add small balls of white for the eyes. Secure the birds on blobs of icing trimmings.

9 Roll out half the white icing to a 10cm (4 inch) circle with a wavy edge. Secure to the roof. From the rest cut out a long thin strip with a wavy edge. Fix around the edges of the board. Use food colouring and a fine paintbrush to paint the birds' features.

DINOSAUR EGG

700g (1½ lb) ready-to-roll icing

purple, yellow, blue and black food colourings

Victoria sandwich cake mixture made with 175g (6oz) flour (see page 14)

½ quantity butter cream (see page 19)

30ml (2 tbsp) clear honey

30.5 x 20.5cm (12 x 8 inch) cake board (optional)

a little royal icing (see page 20)

1 Make the dinosaur at least three days in advance and leave to dry. Colour 125g (4oz) of the ready-to-roll icing purple. Roll one large sausage and a small one about the size of your little finger. Curl them round and pull spikes of icing up on the back. Make the small one pointed at one end for a tail. Cut a slit in one end of the large one for a mouth.

2 It is possible to hire egg-shaped cake moulds; otherwise use two 1.1 litre (2 pint) pudding basins. The mould only needs greasing; the basins should be greased and base-lined. Make the cake mixture and divide between the tins or basins. Bake at 190°C/375°F/gas 5 for 35–40 minutes. Turn out, removing the lining paper, if used, and cool on a wire rack.

3 Colour 125g (4oz) of the remaining ready-to-roll icing yellow and the rest turquoise (by mixing blue and yellow together). Only partly mix in the colouring so that the icing is marbled.

4 The finished egg will lie on its side. Slice off a small piece of cake from one side to prevent the egg wobbling about on the cake board or plate. Halve the cakes horizontally, then sandwich the pieces together with the butter cream.

5 Roll out the turquoise icing. Add 15ml (1 tbsp) water to the honey and heat until boiling; then brush over the egg. Lay the icing over the egg and smooth it to fit. You will need to trim off the excess icing, make a few pleats and smooth over the joins with a palette knife. Tuck the ends underneath the egg. With a sharp knife, cut a zigzag down the middle of the egg, as though it has been cracked open, and ease it apart. Remove one or two of the zigzag points to create space for the dinosaur. Place on the cake board, if using, or a serving plate.

6 Use a little of the yellow icing to make a tongue for the dinosaur and secure inside the mouth. Using a cheese grater, grate the rest of the yellow icing. Pile some into the open crack to represent the inside of the egg, letting it spill over, if liked. Position the dinosaur and the tail in the egg, rearranging the grated icing as necessary. Colour a little royal icing black. Pipe the eyes using white and black royal icing.

SHOOTING STARS

Madeira cake mixture made with 175g (6oz) plain flour (see page 12)

1 quantity butter cream (see page 19)

jam, for filling

33cm (13 inch) round cake board

1kg (2lb 4oz) ready-to-roll icing

dark blue, red, orange, black and silver food colourings

blue and silver floating candles or nightlights

1 Grease and base-line a 3.4 litre (6 pint) ovenproof bowl (see Top Tip on page 142). Make the cake mixture and turn into the bowl, levelling the surface. Bake for about 1½ hours until just firm. Leave to cool in the bowl, then loosen the edges with a palette knife to ease the cake out of the bowl.

2 Slice the dome off the top of the cake so that it sits horizontally into three layers. Sandwich the layers together with half the butter cream and the jam and place on the cake board. Spread with the remaining butter cream.

3 Colour 900g (2lb) of the ready-to-roll icing dark blue, a small ball orange and a small ball red, leaving the remainder white.

4 Use a little of the blue icing to fill any gaps left between the base of the cake and the board. Reserve 225g (8oz) of the icing and roll out the remainder. Use to cover the cake. Dampen the edges of the cake board. Roll out the remaining blue icing and use to cover the edges of the board, trimming off the excess.

5 From the white icing, shape a simple rocket and arrange at an angle on the cake. Shape several round stars and planets in the orange and red icing and secure. Roll some of the red and orange trimmings together to get a marbled effect on one of the planets. Roll out the white icing thinly and cut out a selection of small and large stars. Secure to the cake.

6 Using a fine paintbrush and silver food colouring, paint clusters of smaller stars onto the blue icing. Paint the details on the rocket. Arrange the candles around the cake board.

BALL PIT

Victoria sandwich cake mixture
made with 225g (8oz) flour
(see page 14)

1 quantity butter cream
(see page 19)

jam, for filling

25cm (10 inch) round cake board

red, flesh-coloured (if available),
green, yellow and blue food
colourings

1kg (2lb 4oz) ready-to-roll icing

4 wooden cocktail sticks

1 Make the cake mixture and turn into two prepared 20cm (8 inch) round sandwich tins. Bake for about 30 minutes or until just firm to the touch. Turn out and leave to cool on a wire rack.

2 Sandwich the cakes with half the butter cream and the jam and place on the cake board. Spread with the remaining butter cream.

3 Colour 650g (1lb 7oz) of the ready-to-roll icing red and 100g (3½oz) flesh coloured (see Top Tip). Reserve a small piece of white icing for the socks. Colour 100g (3½oz) blue, then divide the remainder into two and colour green and yellow.

4 Roll out 150g (5oz) of the red icing and use to cover the top of the cake. Measure the circumference of the cake using a piece of string. Roll out the remaining red icing to a long strip the length of the string and 5mm (¼ inch) deeper than the cake. Wrap it around the sides of the cake so that it stands proud around the top, fitting the ends neatly together and smoothing down gently. Roll out some blue icing thinly and use to cover the edges of the cake board, trimming off the excess.

5 Roll 50g (2oz) of the flesh-coloured icing into a ball for the head and secure to the top of the cake with a dampened paintbrush. From the remaining flesh-coloured icing, shape two forearms and two legs. Push a cocktail stick into each limb, then press them down, at a slight angle, into the cake. Shape the white icing into socks and secure to the legs. Roll a very thin strip of yellow icing and cut slits along one side. Wrap around the head for hair.

6 Use the remaining icing to shape the balls. To make them evenly sized, roll out each colour under the palms of your hands into long ropes and cut at regular lengths. Then roll into balls and scatter on top of the cake.

7 Shape and position tiny balls of white for the eyes. Paint the features using a fine paintbrush and food colouring.

TOP TIP
If flesh-coloured food colouring is unavailable, use a dash of red colouring instead, but be very careful not to use too much.

IN THE SWIM

Victoria sandwich cake mixture made with 225g (8oz) flour (see page 14)

1 quantity butter cream (see page 19)

jam, for filling

25cm (10 inch) round cake board

1kg (2lb 4oz) ready-to-roll icing

blue, flesh-coloured (if available), orange and yellow food colourings

1 Make the cake mixture and turn into two prepared sandwich tins. Bake for about 30 minutes until just firm to the touch. Turn out, remove the lining paper and leave to cool on a wire rack.

2 Sandwich the cakes with half the butter cream and the jam and place on the cake board. Reserve 30ml (2 tbsp) of the remaining butter cream, then spread the remainder over the cake.

3 Colour 650g (1lb 7oz) of the ready-to-roll icing blue, 150g (5oz) dark blue, 100g (3½oz) flesh-coloured (see Top Tip on page 164), 75g (3oz) orange and 15g (½oz) yellow.

4 Roll out the light blue icing and use to cover the cake, smoothing it to fit the sides. Trim off the excess icing around the base. Roll out the orange icing thinly and use to cover the edges of the cake board, trimming off the excess.

5 Roll the dark blue icing into a ball and flatten it out neatly to a 9cm (3½ inch) round. Use a 5.5cm (2¼ inch) cutter to cut out the centre. Round off the cut edge with your fingers and place the ring on top of the cake. Roll tiny balls of the orange trimmings and yellow icing and flatten them between your thumb and finger. Secure to the blue ring with a dampened paintbrush.

6 Roll 25g (1oz) of the flesh-coloured icing into an oval shape and fit inside the ring. Roll another 35g (1½oz) into a ball and position for the head. Use a tiny dot of icing for the nose. Roll the remainder into a sausage shape and cut in half. Curve into shape for the swimmer's arms and position over the ring on the cake.

7 Put the reserved butter cream in a piping bag fitted with a writing nozzle and use to pipe hair over the head. Use the remaining butter cream to pipe wavy lines around the ring and to pipe 'bubbles' on the sides of the cake. Paint the facial features using food colouring and a fine paintbrush.

TOP TIP

If you are making this cake for a little boy, make the swimmer in the ring male, with shorter hair.

BEST SPECIAL NOVELTY CAKES

BIRTHDAY BEAR

Madeira cake mixture made with 175g (6oz) plain flour (see page 12)

jam, for filling

1 quantity butter cream (see page 19)

28cm (11 inch) round cake board

1.2kg (2¾lb) ready-to-roll icing

green, purple, orange, red and brown food colourings

icing sugar and cornflour, for dusting

coiled parcel ribbons or streamers

1 metre thin orange ribbon, for base of cake

1 metre wide purple ribbon, for edge of board

1 Make the cake mixture and turn into a prepared 23cm (9 inch) round cake tin. Bake for about 1¾ hours or until the cake is golden and firm to the touch. Leave to cool in the tin then turn out, remove the lining paper and place on a wire rack to cool completely.

2 Cut the cake horizontally into three layers and sandwich together with jam and all but 45ml (3 tbsp) of the butter cream. Place on the cake board and spread thinly with the reserved butter cream.

3 Colour 150g (5oz) of the ready-to-roll icing green, 150g (5oz) purple, 150g (5oz) orange, 100g (3½oz) red and 50g (2oz) brown, leaving the remainder white.

4 Roll out the white icing on a surface lightly dusted with icing sugar and use to cover the cake. Smooth the icing around the sides of the cake using hands dusted with cornflour and trim off the excess around the base.

5 Shape three parcels, one from each of the green, purple and orange icings; position these towards the back of the cake, securing the bases with a lightly dampened paintbrush. Cut long thin strips of red icing and secure around the parcels to resemble ribbon.

6 Roll 15g (½oz) pieces of the coloured icings into balls, then elongate slightly into balloon shapes. Arrange in clusters around the parcels.

7 Shape a small teddy bear from the brown icing. Mould the body, head, ears, arms and legs separately, then assemble using a lightly dampened paintbrush to stick the pieces together, propping the teddy up against one of the parcels. Shape a small snout in brown icing and press onto the face. Shape a party hat in coloured icing and press gently into position. Using a fine paintbrush and brown food colouring, paint features on teddy's face.

8 Lightly dampen the edge of the cake board. Thinly roll out a long strip of orange icing and use to cover the board, trimming off the excess to neaten at the edge.

9 Make more balloon shapes and arrange around the base of the cake. Press a small ball of icing onto the end of each balloon for the knot. Cut lengths of parcel ribbon and taper the ends to a point. Press the tapered end of a ribbon into each balloon. Secure the orange ribbon around the base of the cake and the purple ribbon around the edge of the cake board to finish.

PANDA

Victoria sandwich cake mixture
made with 175g (6oz) flour
(see page 14)

⅔ quantity orange-flavoured
butter cream (see page 19)

18cm (7 inch) round cake board

60ml (4 tbsp) apricot glaze
(see page 17)

1.4kg (3lb) ready-to-roll icing

dark and light green, brown,
yellow and black food colourings

15ml (1 tbsp) lightly beaten egg
white

about 125g (4oz) icing sugar

1 Preheat the oven to 160°C/325°F/gas 3. Grease and base-line a 1.4 litre (2½ pint) pudding basin. In a large bowl, beat together all the ingredients for the cake until smooth. Turn into the basin, level the surface and bake for about 1 hour until firm to the touch. Leave to cool in the basin.

2 Trim the cake so that it sits flat when inverted. Slice the cake horizontally into three layers and sandwich together with the butter cream. Then place on the cake board and brush all over with apricot glaze.

3 Colour 700g (1½lb) of the ready-to-roll icing dark green. Roll it out on a surface dusted with cornflour to a 25cm (10 inch) round. Lay over the cake, easing the icing around the side to eliminate creases and folds. Trim off the excess icing at the base and reserve the trimmings.

4 To make the panda, roll 225g (8oz) icing into a ball for the body. Stand it on the work surface and elongate the top of the ball slightly. Roll another 50g (2oz) for the head and secure to the body, using a dampened paintbrush. Pinch the front of the head to a point to make a snout. Use another 25g (1oz) for each leg and 15g (½oz) for each arm. Shape and secure. Use a little more icing to shape the ears and secure to the head.

5 Beat the egg white in a bowl, gradually adding the icing sugar until softly peaking. Lightly dampen the panda and brush with the icing to make fur. Reserve the remaining icing. Place a dampened piece of cling film directly onto the surface of the icing to prevent it drying out.

6 Colour half the ready-to-roll icing different shades of green, a quarter brown and a quarter yellow. Roll out each colour separately and cut out small leaf shapes between 2.5cm (1 inch) and 5cm (2 inches) long. Lay the leaves over a foil-covered rolling pin and wooden spoon. Make a small brown twig and set everything aside, with the panda, for 24 hours to set.

7 Paint the panda with black food colouring. Secure a few small leaves onto the twig. Position the panda on the cake. Place a little icing in a piping bag fitted with a fine writing nozzle and use to pipe claws. Colour the remaining icing green and use to secure leaves around the panda and cake board.

> **TOP TIP**
> If necessary, dull bright green colouring with a little black or brown for more realistic leaves.

ANIMAL FARM

Madeira cake mixture made
with 175g (6oz) plain flour
(see page 12)

jam, for filling

1 quantity butter cream
(see page 19)

23cm (9 inch) square cake board

green, brown, pink and yellow
food colourings

icing sugar and cornflour, for
dusting

1.5 metres green cord or ribbon

1 Make the cake mixture and turn into a prepared 20cm (8 inch) square cake tin. Bake for about 1¾ hours or until the cake is golden and firm to the touch. Leave to cool in the tin then turn out, remove the lining paper and place on a wire rack to cool completely.

2 Cut the cake horizontally into three layers and sandwich together with jam and all but 45ml (3 tbsp) of the butter cream. Place the cake on the board and cover thinly with the reserved butter cream.

3 Colour 700g (1lb 9oz) of the ready-to-roll icing light green, 75g (3oz) dark green, 225g (8oz) dark brown, 50g (2oz) light brown, 50g (2oz) pink and 50g (2oz) yellow, leaving the remainder white.

4 Roll out the light green icing on a surface dusted with icing sugar and use to cover the cake. Smooth the icing around the sides of the cake using hands dusted with cornflour and trim off the excess around the base.

5 Roll out the dark brown icing to a 19 x 14cm (7½ x 5½ inch) rectangle and cut in half lengthways. Cut out a heart or small window shape in each piece, towards the top. Secure the icing on top of the cake so the sides sit on the edges of the cake. Mark lines 1cm (½ inch) apart down the brown strips.

6 Shape two pig faces from the pink icing. Start with a round ball and flatten to make a face. Add a snout, indenting the nostrils with a cocktail stick, and ears. Texture a flattened ball of white icing with a cocktail stick for the sheep's head, then add an oval face and ears in light brown icing. Position two small white eyes.

7 Use a large oval shape in yellow icing for the cow's face and add small ears. Shape the snout and horns in light brown, then two small white eyes. Shape the horse's face from white icing, adding ears and eyes; indent the nostrils with a cocktail stick. Use strips of green icing for reins and light brown icing for the mane.

8 Using a fine paintbrush and black or brown food colouring, paint the features onto the animals, then paint a small spider and web in one of the stable windows.

9 Dampen the top edges of the cake board. Roll out the dark green icing and use to cover the board, trimming off the excess along the edges. From the remaining green and yellow icings, cut out grass shapes and secure along the front edge, then position a tiny mouse. Tie the decorative cord around the base of the cake.

FOOTBALL MAD

Madeira cake mixture made
with 225g (8oz) plain flour
(see page 12)

1 quantity butter cream
(see page 19)

jam, for filling

30cm (12 inch) round cake board

1.5kg (3lb 6oz) ready-to-roll icing

black, green and red food
colourings

1 Grease and base-line a 3.4 litre (6 pint) ovenproof bowl (see Top Tip on page 142). Make the cake mixture, turn into the bowl and level the surface. Bake for about 1½ hours or until just firm. Cool in the bowl.

2 Slice the dome off the top of the cake so that it sits on the surface, then cut the cake horizontally into three layers. Sandwich with half the butter cream and the jam and place on the cake board. Spread with the remaining butter cream. Colour 175g (6oz) of the ready-to-roll icing black, 150g (5oz) green and 75g (3oz) red, leaving the remainder white.

3 Roll out 450g (1lb) of the white icing thinly and use to cover the cake, smoothing the sides and trimming off the excess. (Don't worry about getting a perfect finish; the icing will be covered.)

4 Roll out half the black icing and half the remaining white icing. Make a cardboard template of a hexagon and cut hexagon shapes out of the icing. Lightly dampen the cake surface and secure the hexagons to the top of the cake, shaping the pattern so that each black hexagon is surrounded by white hexagons. Continue covering the cake with the shapes, using the remaining icing as you work down the sides. (The shapes become slightly more difficult to fit as you work around the sides, but ease them into place and trim where you need to.)

5 Roll out the green icing thinly and use to cover the edge of the cake board, trimming off the excess. If liked, use the green icing trimmings to shape grass and secure around the base of the ball.

6 For the rosette, roll out the red icing and cut out a long thin strip. Pleat it up slightly as you form it into a round and secure to the side of the football. Shape two ribbons and arrange them to one side, then position a circle of red icing in the middle.

TOP TIP
Vary the colours of the football and the rosette to match the recipient's favourite football team colours.

TRAIN CAKE

325g (11oz) self-raising white flour

5ml (1 tsp) baking powder

225g (8oz) unsalted butter or margarine, softened

4 medium eggs

10ml (2 tsp) vanilla essence

jam, for filling

1 quantity butter cream
(see page 19)

20cm (8 inch) round cake board

750g (1lb 10oz) ready-to-roll icing

blue, green and red food colourings

icing sugar, for dusting

0.75 metre green ribbon

selection of liquorice sweets

birthday candles

1 Grease and line a deep 15cm (6 inch) round cake tin. Sift the flour and baking powder into a bowl. Add the butter or margarine, sugar, eggs and vanilla essence and beat with an electric whisk for about 2 minutes until creamy.

2 Turn half the mixture into the prepared tin and level the surface. Bake at 170°C/325°F/gas 3 for about 1 hour until firm, then transfer to a wire rack to cool. Clean and re-line the tin, then bake the remaining mixture in the same way; turn out and cool.

3 Cut each cake horizontally into two layers. Sandwich all the layers together with the jam and all but 45ml (3 tbsp) of the butter cream. Place the cake on the board and spread thinly with the reserved butter cream.

4 Colour 450g (1lb) of the ready-to-roll icing pale blue, 125g (4oz) green and 125g (4oz) red, leaving the remainder white. Roll out a quarter of the pale blue icing on a surface dusted with icing sugar and cut out a 15cm (6 inch) circle. Fit on the top of the cake.

5 Measure the circumference of the cake with a piece of string. Roll out the remaining blue icing to a strip the length of the string and depth of the cake. Roll up lightly and position against the side of the cake, then unroll the icing around the side to cover it. Using hands dusted with icing sugar, smooth the icing around the join at the top edge.

6 Dampen the cake board and the icing at the base of the cake. Roll out the green icing to a long curved strip, about 48cm (18 inches) long and 5cm (2 inches) wide. Cut an uneven, wavy line along the inner edge. Fit the strip around the base of the cake so the wavy edge sits over the blue icing and the outer edge covers the board. Trim off the icing around the edge of the board. Secure the ribbon around the edge of the board.

7 To make the trains, thinly roll out the red icing. Cut out two inverted 'L' shapes for the engines, approximately 3cm (1¼ inches) high and 5cm (2 inches) long. Position on opposite sides of the cake, just above the green icing. To make the trucks, cut out four or six 4 x 2.5cm (1½ x 1 inch) rectangles. Secure these behind the engines.

8 Cut the wheels, windows and funnels from the liquorice sweets. Finely chop some sweets for the cargo in the trucks. Dampen the sweets and press into position.

9 Thinly roll the white icing and cut out little cloud shapes in various sizes. Secure above the train and on top of the cake. Position the candles on top.

SLEEPY RAG DOLL

Madeira cake mixture made with 125g (4oz) plain flour (see page 12)

1 quantity butter cream (see page 19)

jam, for filling

800g (1lb 12oz) ready-to-roll icing

brown, red, green and yellow food colourings

25cm (10 inch) round cake board

1 Grease and line a 900g (2lb) loaf tin. Make the cake mixture and turn into the tin. Bake for about 1¼ hours until golden and just firm to the touch. Leave to cool in the tin.

2 Colour 350g (12oz) of the icing light brown, 225g (8oz) red, 100g (3½oz) light green, 50g (2oz) pale pink, 25g (1oz) dark green and 25g (1oz) yellow, leaving the rest white.

3 On a piece of greaseproof paper, draw around the end of the loaf tin. Extend the sides by 2.5cm (1 inch) then join the curve to make the headboard template. Roll out a little brown icing and cut a headboard. Leave to harden for 2–3 days.

4 Dampen the cake board. Roll out two-thirds of the red icing and cover the board. Slice the domed top off the cake; cut horizontally into three. Sandwich with half the butter cream and some jam. Spread the remaining butter cream over the top and sides. Roll out the remaining brown icing and cover the sides and one end of the cake. Place the cake on the cake board.

5 Roll out a red bottom sheet 14 x 6cm (5½ x 2½ inches). Reserve the trimmings. Dampen the top end of the cake and secure the sheet in place. Shape a pillow in white icing and secure on the red sheet. Shape a ball of pale pink icing and place on the pillow. Add a tiny blob of pink icing for the nose. Make a body shape in pink icing and place on the cake.

6 Roll out the light green icing to a 17cm (6½ inch) square for the blanket. Roll out tiny balls of white and dark green icing and roll into the light green icing. Trim the edges. Drape the blanket over the bed. Roll out a strip of dark green icing, for the top edge.

7 Roll out the yellow icing into a rope, then plait. Secure to the doll's head. Make a yellow fringe and closed eyes. Add a mouth shaped from the red icing trimmings.

8 Dampen the top end of the cake. Press the headboard into position. Add two balls of red icing at each end of the headboard. Shape and secure red ribbons onto the plaits. Finish the cake by painting two rosy cheeks with diluted red food colouring.

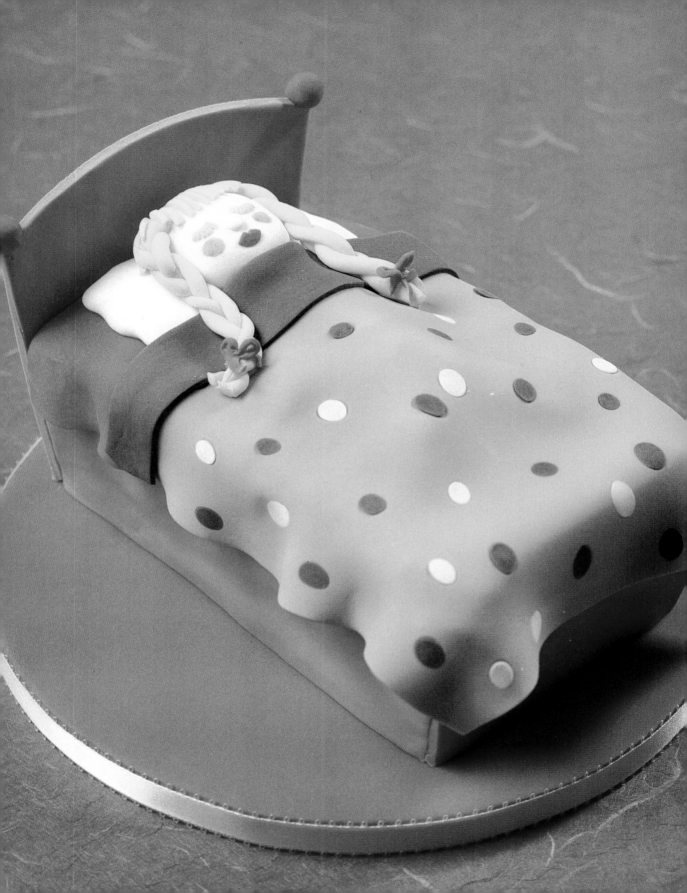

FLOWERPOT

Madeira cake mixture made
with 125g (4oz) plain flour
(see page 12)

½ quantity butter cream
(see page 19)

jam, for filling

900g (2lb) ready-to-roll icing

red, brown, green, orange and
pink food colourings

18cm (7 inch) round cake board

Smarties

1 Grease and line the base and sides of a terracotta flowerpot measuring 12cm (4½ inches) deep and 13cm (5 inches) across the top. Grease and base-line a 600ml (1 pint) ovenproof bowl (see Top Tip on page 142). Make the cake mixture and turn it into the pot and bowl. Bake, allowing about 45 minutes for the bowl and 1 hour for the pot. Leave to cool in the containers.

2 Colour 500g (1lb 2oz) of the ready-to-roll icing terracotta colour using about one part red colouring to two parts brown. Colour 200g (7oz) dark green, 75g (3oz) orange, 75g (3oz) pink, leaving the remainder white. Lightly dampen the cake board. Roll out some green icing and use to cover the board, trimming off the excess around the edges.

3 Slice the flowerpot cake horizontally into three and sandwich half with the butter cream and the jam. Spread a little more butter cream around the sides of the cake. Reserve 50g (2oz) of the terracotta icing and roll out the remainder to a long, slightly curved strip, about 11cm (4½ inches) wide and about 35cm (14 inches) long. Roll the cake in the strip, trimming off the excess where the ends meet. Reserve the trimmings.

4 Transfer the cake to the board. Roll out the terracotta trimmings to a long strip, about 2.5cm (1 inch) wide and the circumference of the top of the cake. Dampen the top edge of the cake with water and secure the strip in position.

5 Trim the smaller cake so it sits comfortably inside the rim of the base and spread with the remaining butter cream. Roll out the remaining green icing and use to cover the cake.

6 Roll out a little of the orange, pink and white icing and cut out flowers using a cutter, about 5cm (2 inches) in diameter. Press gently onto the cake securing with a dampened paintbrush. Press a Smartie into the centre of each flower as you work. Roll out the remaining icing and use to cover the rest of the cake with flowers.

KEYBOARD

Madeira cake mixture made with 175g (6oz) plain flour (see page 12)

½ quantity butter cream (see page 19)

rectangular board or tray, measuring at least 40 x 25cm (16 x 10 inches)

1.3kg (3lb) ready-to-roll icing

black, blue, purple and red food colourings

1 Make the cake mixture and turn into a prepared 18cm (7 inch) square cake tin. Bake for about 1½ hours or until the cake is golden and just firm to the touch. Leave to cool in the tin.

2 Cut the dome off the top of the cake, then halve the cake horizontally. Place the two pieces side by side on the board, securing the ends together with butter cream. Cut a 26 x 9cm (10½ x 3½ inch) rectangle out of the front side of the cake, about 1cm (½ inch) deep. Spread the cake with the remaining butter cream. Colour 825g (1lb 13oz) of the ready-to-roll icing black, 200g (7oz) blue, 50g (2oz) purple and a tiny piece red, leaving the remainder white.

3 Reserve 150g (5oz) of the black icing. Roll out the remainder and use to cover the top and sides of the cake, smoothing down the icing around the sides and trimming off the excess. Flatten and smooth the icing as much as possible and accentuate the edges as corners with your fingers.

4 Roll out the white icing to a 24 x 7cm (9½ x 2¾ inch) rectangle, trimming the edges as neatly as possible. Lift into position over the cut-out area of the cake. Mark the white keys with a knife.

5 Roll more black icing to a 5mm (¼ inch) thickness and then cut out 4.5cm x 5mm (1¾ x ¼ inch) pieces. Position over the white keys securing with water.

6 From the remaining black icing, cut out a speaker panel and mark lines over it using the back of a knife. Position on the left-hand side of the cake. Position another black panel across the top of the cake, adding a smaller purple panel over this. Use more icing trimmings to add small controls.

7 Using a fine paintbrush and food colouring, paint words on the panel. Lightly dampen the board. Roll out the blue icing and use to cover the board, trimming off the excess around the edges.

CD PLAYER

Victoria sandwich cake mixture
made with 225g (8oz) flour
(see page 14)

1 quantity butter cream
(see page 19)

30cm (12 inch) square cake board

750g (1lb 10oz) ready-to-roll icing

yellow, black, purple, silver and
brown food colourings

1 liquorice Catherine wheel

1 Grease and line a 15cm (6 inch) square cake tin and a 25cm (10 inch) square tin or large roasting tin. Make the cake mixture and turn a 1cm (½ inch) depth of mixture into the small tin, then the remainder into the large tin. Bake at 180°C/350°F/gas 4 for 20–25 minutes until just firm. Leave to cool in the tins.

2 Using a knife, round off two of the corners on the small cake to make a CD player shape. Square off the sides of the larger cake if made in a roasting tin and put on the cake board. Spread with three-quarters of the butter cream. Colour 375g (13oz) of the ready-to-roll icing yellow, 250g (9oz) black and 125g (4oz) purple.

3 Roll out the yellow icing and use to cover the cake on the board, trimming off the excess around the base. Using a 10cm (4 inch) cutter or small bowl as a guide, mark a CD outline on the icing, then carefully mark a semi-circle for another CD underneath it.

4 Spread the small cake with the remaining butter cream. Reserve 50g (2oz) of the black icing. Roll out the remainder and use to cover the cake, trimming off the excess around the base. Slide a fish slice under the cake and position it on the yellow base.

5 Use the reserved black icing to shape the features of the player, starting with the lid, then the controls, securing with a dampened paintbrush. Lightly dampen the cake board. Roll out the purple icing and use to cover the board, trimming off the excess around the edges.

6 Use the silver, black and brown colourings to paint the discs and features on the player.

7 Unroll the liquorice and cut in half. Shape two small ear pieces in black icing trimmings and press a piece of liquorice into each. Tuck the ends of the liquorice into the back of the player.

SWEET CROWN

Madeira cake mixture made
with 175g (6oz) plain flour
(see page 12)

1 quantity butter cream
(see page 19)

jam, for filling

25cm (10 inch) round cake board

1.25kg (2lb 12oz) ready-to-roll
icing

purple, green and red food
colourings

½ quantity royal icing
(see page 20)

3 metres fine gold braid

1 metre purple velvet ribbon, for
edge of board

a selection of brightly coloured
boiled sweets and foil-wrapped
chocolates

1 Make the cake mixture and turn into a prepared 20cm (8 inch) round tin. Bake for 1½ hours or until the cake is golden and just firm to the touch. Leave to cool in the tin.

2 Halve the cake horizontally and sandwich with half the butter cream and jam. Place on the cake board and spread with the remaining butter cream. Colour 650g (1lb 7oz) of the ready-to-roll icing green, 75g (3oz) red and the remainder purple.

3 Roll out the green icing and use to cover the cake, smoothing it to fit around the sides. Trim off the excess icing around the base.

4 Measure the circumference of the cake with string. Cut out greaseproof paper that length and 2.5cm (1 inch) deeper than the cake. Roll out the purple icing and trim to the same size. Slide the paper under the icing strip. Using a sharp knife, cut a zigzag line along one edge, no deeper than 2.5cm (1 inch) into the strip.

5 Dampen the sides of the cake. Lift the strip and secure it around the sides of the cake. Leave the paper in place, sealing the ends together with sticky tape. Leave in a cool, dry place for 1–2 days until the icing is set, then remove the paper collar.

6 Dampen the edges of the cake board. Roll out the red icing and use to cover the edges.

7 Put the royal icing in a piping bag fitted with a writing nozzle. Unwrap some of the boiled sweets and secure around the sides of the cake at regular intervals using a little of the royal icing. Pipe some icing around one sweet and in a curvy line to the next sweet. Secure the gold braid around the sweet and over the piped line. Continue piping more lines and securing the braid all round the cake. Secure the remaining braid around the base of the cake and the purple ribbon around the edge of the cake board. Before serving, pile sweets into the centre of the cake.

TOP TIP
This cake can be decorated a week or two in advance, but leave the side decoration until only a couple of days before the party as boiled sweets soften once unwrapped.

BEST CELEBRATION CAKES

TIERED CELEBRATION CAKE

Makes 80–100 slices

Preparation: 2–3 hours, plus standing

Cooking time: large cake 4 hours; small cake 2½–3 hours

Freezing: not recommended

355–285 cals per slice

2 round rich fruit cakes, 23cm (9 inches) and 15cm (6 inches) (see page 15)

30cm (12 inch) round cake board

100g (3½oz) apricot glaze (see page 17)

1.5kg (3¼lb) almond paste (see page 17)

icing sugar, to dust

900g (2lb) royal icing (see page 20)

TO DECORATE

30–40 small edible flowers, such as primulas, primroses, violets, apple blossom or herb flowers

a little lightly beaten egg white, for brushing

caster sugar, for dusting

450g (1lb) small fresh strawberries

0.75 metre fine white muslin

2 metres fine white ribbon or paper cord

1 Place the large cake on the cake board and brush generously with apricot glaze. Lightly knead two-thirds of the almond paste on a surface dusted with icing sugar and roll out to a 35cm (14 inch) round. Lift the almond paste over the cake and ease it to fit around the side; trim off any excess around the base.

2 Position the small cake centrally on top and brush with more apricot glaze. Roll out the remaining almond paste to a 28cm (11 inch) round and use to cover the small cake.

3 Set aside a little royal icing for securing the decorations. Using a palette knife, spread some royal icing over the small cake, covering in an even layer and spreading until fairly smooth. Cover the large cake in the same way, then cover the cake board with a thin layer of icing. Leave to dry.

4 To make the sugared flowers, brush both sides of the petals with a little beaten egg white, then sprinkle generously with caster sugar. Shake off excess sugar and place the flowers on a sheet of greaseproof paper. Leave for several hours or overnight to dry. Sugar the strawberries in the same way and leave to dry for 1–2 hours.

5 Cut the fine white muslin into two long strips, one measuring 75 x 20cm (30 x 8 inches), the other 63 x 20cm (25 x 8 inches). Using short lengths of ribbon or cord, tie each strip tightly at regular intervals to form 5 or 6 even-sized swags.

6 Place the longer muslin strip around the top edge of the large cake, securing at the ties with a dot of icing. (If the muslin falls away from the cake, prop up with cocktail sticks until the icing has dried.) Secure the shorter strip around the top of the small cake.

7 Scatter caster sugar over the muslin and around the base of the cake board. Using more icing, secure the flowers and strawberries on top of the cake and around the edges. Store in a cool place until ready to serve.

TOP TIP

Sugared flowers can be made up to 2 weeks in advance and stored in an airtight container. Don't arrange the strawberries until the day, just in case the juices run.

CELEBRATION GÂTEAU

Makes 40 slices
Preparation: 1¼ hours, plus soaking
and leaves
Cooking time: 1¾ hours
Freezing: suitable (stage 3)
460 cals per slice

225g (8oz) raisins

75ml (5 tbsp) brandy

150g (5oz) walnuts

65g (2½oz) preserved stem ginger
in syrup, drained

550ml (18fl oz) milk

30ml (2 tbsp) wine vinegar

300g (10oz) plain chocolate

225g (8oz) soft margarine

575g (1¼lb) caster sugar

5 eggs

800g (1¾lb) self-raising white
flour

65g (2½oz) cocoa powder

15ml (1 tbsp) bicarbonate of soda

25ml (5 tsp) mixed spice

150ml (¼ pint) ginger wine

ALMOND PASTE
175g (6oz) ground almonds

75g (3oz) unsalted butter

90ml (6 tbsp) preserved stem
ginger syrup

ICING
350g (12oz) plain chocolate

60ml (4 tbsp) liquid glucose

2 egg whites

about 900g (2lb) icing sugar

TO DECORATE
about 125g (4oz) chocolate for
the leaves

edible gold lustre powder
(optional)

1 Preheat the oven to 160°C/325°F/gas 3. Grease and line a 25cm (10 inch) and 15cm (6 inch) cake tin. Soak the raisins in the brandy for 2–3 hours or overnight. Chop the walnuts and ginger. Mix together the milk and vinegar. Break up the chocolate and melt in a heatproof bowl set over a pan of simmering water.

2 Put the margarine, sugar and eggs in a very large bowl. Sift the flour, cocoa powder, bicarbonate of soda and spice into the bowl. Add half the milk mixture and beat until smooth. Add the melted chocolate and remaining milk and stir until smooth. Stir in the raisins, walnuts and ginger.

3 Divide between the prepared tins. Bake the small cake for 1–1¼ hours and the large cake for 1¾ hours or until a skewer inserted into the centre comes out clean. Leave to cool in the tins, then drizzle with the ginger wine.

4 For the almond paste, beat the ground almonds, softened butter and syrup together in a bowl until smooth. Using a palette knife, spread in a thin layer over both cakes. Place the large cake on a board or plate.

5 For the icing, melt the chocolate with the glucose in a large heatproof bowl as above; cool slightly. Gradually beat in more icing sugar, using an electric whisk. When the icing becomes too stiff to beat, turn it onto a work surface and knead in enough icing sugar to make a stiff paste.

6 Roll out a generous two-thirds of the icing paste on a surface dusted with icing sugar. Lift over the large cake and smooth over the top and sides, using your hands dusted with icing sugar. Cover the small cake with the remaining icing and carefully position on top of the larger cake.

7 Make a selection of chocolate leaves (see stages 8–9 on page 42) and decorate the cake with the leaves, to serve. If desired, sprinkle the cake with a little gold lustre powder for a festive touch.

LUXURY CHRISTMAS CAKE

Makes 30–40 slices
Preparation: 1 hour, plus macerating
Cooking time: 3–4 hours
Freezing: suitable (stage 5)
315–235 cals per slice

1 lemon

1 orange

225g (8oz) dried apricots

175g (6oz) stoned prunes

175g (6oz) unblanched almonds

175g (6oz) glacé cherries

225g (8oz) currants

125g (4oz) sultanas

225g (8oz) raisins

150ml (¼ pint) brandy, rum, porter or sweet stout

125g (4oz) chopped candied peel

350g (12oz) self-raising white flour

10ml (2 tsp) mixed spice

300g (10oz) unsalted butter, softened

300g (10oz) soft dark muscovado sugar

6 eggs, beaten

60ml (4 tbsp) treacle

TO DECORATE
apricot glaze (see page 17)

450g (1lb) almond paste
(see page 17)

450g (1lb) ready-to-roll icing, plus an extra 450g (1lb) for stars

5ml (1 tsp) gum tragacanth

edible gold lustre powder

gold and silver food colouring

a little royal icing (see page 20)

1 Grate the rind from the lemon and orange and squeeze the juice. Roughly chop the apricots, prunes and almonds. Wash, dry and halve the cherries. Mix the apricots, prunes and citrus rinds and juices together in a large bowl, with the currants, sultanas and raisins. Add the brandy (or other liquor), cover and leave to macerate overnight, stirring occasionally.

2 The next day, preheat the oven to 160°C/325°F/gas 3. Line a 25cm (10 inch) round or 23cm (9 inch) square cake tin with a double or triple layer of greaseproof paper. Grease with butter.

3 Add the cherries, nuts and peel to the macerated fruit mixture and stir well. Sift the flour, spice and 2.5ml (½ tsp) salt together. In a large bowl, cream together the butter and sugar until fluffy. Gradually beat in the eggs, beating well between each addition to prevent curdling. Stir in the treacle, then fold in the flour and fruit.

4 Spoon the mixture into the cake tin, level the surface, then make a slight hollow in the middle. Bake in the preheated oven for 1 hour, then reduce the temperature to 140°C/275°F/gas 1 and bake for a further 2–3 hours. Cover the top of the cake with buttered paper if browning too much. Test by inserting a skewer into the centre of the cake – if it comes out clean, the cake is cooked.

5 Leave in the tin until cool enough to handle, then turn out onto a wire rack to cool completely in the paper. When cold, keep one layer of the greaseproof paper on the cake, then wrap in foil. Store in a cool dry place.

6 Up to one week before Christmas, set the cake up on a board. Brush the cake with apricot glaze and cover with almond paste. Leave to dry for 24 hours, then cover with ready-to-roll icing (see page 22).

7 For the decorations, knead the ready-to-roll icing until pliable, then knead in the gum tragacanth (which will help the icing to dry and harden). Using a star-shaped cutter, stamp out stars from icing rolled to a thickness of about 3mm (⅛ inch). Place on a baking tray lined with non-stick parchment paper. Sprinkle a little edible gold lustre powder on a plate and press some of the stars gently onto it. Leave the stars to dry for 24 hours. When hardened, paint some of the stars with gold or silver food colouring. Arrange the stars on the newly iced cake, pushing them lightly into the icing. If necessary, fix them in place with a little royal icing.

CANDLELIT CHRISTMAS CAKE

Makes 24–30 slices
Preparation: 1 hour, plus standing
Cooking time: about 2½ hours
Freezing: suitable (stage 4)
715–575 cals per slice

225g (8oz) each of ready-to-eat dried apricots, dried pears and sultanas

40g (1½oz) chopped glacé ginger

60ml (4 tbsp) brandy

400g (14oz) unsalted butter, softened

400g (14oz) caster sugar

4 eggs

350g (12oz) plain white flour

5ml (1 tsp) baking powder

15ml (1 tsp) vanilla essence

110g (4oz) ground almonds

50g (2oz) blanched almonds, chopped

50g (2oz) hazelnuts, chopped

TO FINISH
30cm (12 inch) silver round cake board

60ml (4 tbsp) apricot glaze (see page 17)

1kg (2¼lb) ready-made white almond paste

icing sugar, for dusting

1kg (2¼lb) ready-to-roll icing

cornflour, for dusting

6 large sprigs of fresh bay leaves

1 egg white, lightly beaten

caster sugar, for sprinkling

6 nightlights

2 metres fine silver cord

1 metre thick silver cord

1 Roughly chop the dried apricots and pears in a food processor. Place in a bowl with the sultanas, glacé ginger and brandy, stir to mix well and leave to stand for about 30 minutes.

2 Grease and line a deep 23cm (9 inch) round cake tin. Tie a double thickness of brown paper around the outside of the tin (see Protecting a Fruit Cake on page 9).

3 Cream the butter and sugar together in a large bowl. Gradually beat in the eggs, adding a little of the flour to prevent curdling. Sift the remaining flour and baking powder together over the mixture, then fold in. Add the soaked fruits, vanilla essence, ground almonds and chopped nuts; stir until evenly combined.

4 Turn the mixture into the prepared tin and bake at 150°C/300°F/gas 2 for about 2½ hours until a skewer inserted into the centre of the cake comes out clean. Leave to cool in the tin, then turn out onto a wire rack and leave until cold.

5 Place the cake on the cake board and brush with apricot glaze. Cover with the almond paste. Leave in a cool dry place for 1–2 days before applying the icing.

6 Roll out the icing on a surface lightly dusted with cornflour and use to cover the cake (see page 22).

7 Wash the bay leaves and dry on kitchen paper. Brush with the egg white, then sprinkle generously with sugar. Leave on a wire rack to dry for several hours.

8 Arrange the nightlights in a circle on top of the cake, 1cm (½ inch) from the edge. Press the bay leaves into the icing around the candles, then trail the fine silver cord around the leaves. Secure the thick silver cord around the base of the cake. When ready to serve, light the nightlights.

COCONUT GÂTEAU WITH LIME AND KIRSCH

Makes 10–12 slices
Preparation: 45 minutes, plus cooling
Cooking time: 30 minutes
Freezing: suitable (stage 2)
515–430 cals per slice

7 egg whites

good pinch of salt

5ml (1 tsp) cream of tartar

10ml (2 tsp) vanilla essence

300g (10oz) caster sugar

finely grated rind of 2 limes

50g (2oz) freshly grated coconut,
or desiccated coconut

125g (4oz) plain white flour

TO DECORATE
4 limes

50g (2oz) caster sugar

60ml (4 tbsp) Kirsch

125g (4oz) piece fresh coconut, or
coconut shreds

450ml (¾ pint) double cream

45ml (3 tbsp) icing sugar

175g (6oz) Greek yogurt

1 Preheat the oven to 160°C/325°F/gas 3. Grease and base-line two 20cm (8 inch) sandwich tins. Whisk the egg whites in a large bowl until just holding their shape. Add the salt and cream of tartar and whisk until stiff but not dry. Gradually whisk in the sugar, a little at a time, whisking well between each addition until stiff and very shiny. Whisk in the lime rind with the last of the sugar.

2 Add the coconut, then sift in the flour and lightly fold in until just incorporated. Divide between the tins and level the surfaces. Bake for 30 minutes until the surfaces are pale golden and crusty. Leave the cakes to cool in the tins.

3 For the decoration, finely pare the rind from two of the limes in shreds, using a sharp knife. Remove the peel and white pith from all the limes, then thinly slice the flesh. Dissolve the sugar in 150ml (¼ pint) water in a small heavy-based pan over a low heat. Add the lime slices and shredded rind and cook gently for 1 minute. Drain with a slotted spoon and reserve. Leave the syrup to cool.

4 Stir the Kirsch into the cooled syrup. Split each cake in half horizontally and drizzle each layer with the syrup. If using fresh coconut, cut away the skin, then pare the flesh using a swivel vegetable peeler. Lightly toast the parings of coconut shreds until turning golden.

5 Whip the cream with the icing sugar until just peaking, then fold in the yogurt. Place one cake layer on a serving plate and spread with a little of the cream mixture. Arrange a quarter of the lime slices on top and sprinkle with a little of the coconut shavings. Repeat the layers twice, using up half the cream and most of the coconut and lime slices.

6 Top with the final cake layer and spread the remaining cream over the cake. Decorate the top with the remaining lime slices and coconut, and the pared lime rind. Chill until ready to serve.

HAZELNUT MERINGUE GÂTEAU

Makes 10 slices
Preparation: 40 minutes, plus cooling
Cooking time: about 1½ hours
Freezing: not suitable
630 cals per slice

MERINGUE
125g (4oz) shelled hazelnuts

5 egg whites

250g (9oz) caster sugar

2.5ml (½ tsp) ground mixed spice

75g (3oz) white chocolate, chopped

75g (3oz) plain chocolate, chopped

TO FINISH
75g (3oz) shelled hazelnuts

125g (4oz) caster sugar

300ml (½ pint) double cream

cocoa powder, for dusting (optional)

1 Line two baking sheets with non-stick baking parchment. Draw a 23cm (9 inch) circle onto one sheet, using a plate as a guide. On the other sheet, draw a 17.5cm (6½ inch) circle. Turn the paper over. Preheat the oven to 140°C/275°F/gas 1.

2 To make the meringue, lightly toast the hazelnuts, then chop roughly. Whisk the egg whites in a bowl until stiff but not dry. Gradually whisk in the sugar, a tablespoon at a time, whisking well between each addition until stiff and very shiny. Whisk in the spice with the last of the sugar. Carefully fold in the chopped hazelnuts and white and plain chocolate.

3 Spoon the meringue onto the circles, then spread neatly into rounds. Bake for about 1½ hours until dry and the undersides are firm when tapped. Turn the oven off and leave the meringues to cool in the oven.

4 Lightly oil a baking sheet. Put the hazelnuts in a small heavy-based pan with the sugar. Cook over a gentle heat stirring, until the sugar melts. Continue cooking until the mixture caramelises to a rich golden brown colour, then pour onto the baking sheet. Leave to cool and harden.

5 Place the praline in a polythene bag and beat with a rolling pin until very coarsely crushed.

6 Carefully transfer the largest meringue round to a serving plate. Whip the cream until softly peaking, then spread over the meringue. Scatter the praline onto the cream, reserving a little for the top of the meringue, if liked. Cover with the smaller meringue round and scatter with the reserved praline or, if preferred, dust the top of the gâteau with a generous sprinkling of cocoa powder.

TOP TIP
Switch the baking sheets around halfway through cooking the meringue rounds to ensure an even result.

TIERED FRUIT GÂTEAU

Makes 24 slices
Preparation: 1½ hours, plus cooling
Cooking time: 45–50 minutes
Freezing: suitable (without glazed
fruits)
425 cals per slice

LARGE CAKE
6 eggs
175g (6oz) caster sugar
175g (6oz) plain white flour

SMALL CAKE
2 eggs
50g (2oz) caster sugar
50g (2oz) plain white flour

FILLING
350g (12oz) strawberries
175g (6oz) raspberries
30ml (2 tbsp) rosewater
40g (1½oz) caster sugar

TO FINISH
175g (6oz) shelled hazelnuts
150g (5oz) caster sugar
900ml (1½ pints) double cream
350g (12oz) plain or white
chocolate
900g (2lb) mixture soft fruits,
such as strawberries, raspberries,
blueberries, red and blackcurrants
105ml (7 tbsp) redcurrant jelly
sprigs of flowering rosemary or
other flowers

1 Preheat the oven to 180°C/350°F/gas 4. Grease and base-line two round cake tins, one 28cm (11 inches) and the other 15cm (6 inches). Dust with flour and shake out the excess.

2 For the large cake, whisk the eggs and sugar together in a very large heatproof bowl over a pan of hot water until the mixture is thick enough to leave a trail. Remove the bowl from the pan and whisk until cooled. Sift the flour over the mixture and fold in lightly. Turn into the large tin and bake for 20–25 minutes until just firm. Cool on a wire rack. Make the small cake in the same way and bake for 15–17 minutes.

3 Slice the strawberries and toss in a bowl with the raspberries, rosewater and sugar. Gently heat the hazelnuts and sugar in a heavy-based pan with 15ml (1 tbsp) water until the sugar dissolves, then cook to a deep brown caramel. Immediately pour onto an oiled baking sheet. Leave to cool and harden, then coarsely crush. Whip the cream until just peaking, then fold in the praline.

4 Halve the cakes horizontally. Sandwich the large cakes together on a platter with two-thirds of the fruit filling and a little praline cream. Sandwich the small cake with the remaining fruits and a little more cream. Cut a strip of greaseproof paper, 5cm (2 inches) longer than the circumference of the large cake and 2cm (¾ inch) deeper. Repeat for the small cake.

5 Spread the remaining praline cream over the cakes, then carefully position the small cake, off-centre, on the large one. Chill.

6 Melt the chocolate in a bowl over a pan of simmering water. Spread over each greaseproof strip, right to the long edges and 1cm (½ inch) from each end. Leave until the chocolate has thickened slightly, then carefully wrap the small strip around the small cake. Wrap the long strip around the large cake. Chill for 5–10 minutes until set, then carefully peel away the paper.

7 Decorate the gâteau with the fruits, halving any large strawberries. Melt the redcurrant jelly with 15ml (1 tbsp) water and brush over the fruits. Finally, arrange sprigs of flowering rosemary or other flowers on top.

CELEBRATION CAKE

Makes 40 slices
Preparation: 1½ hours, plus standing
Cooking time: 3½–4 hours
Freezing: suitable (stage 2)
420 cals per slice

150g (5oz) glacé cherries

1.5kg (3lb) mixed dried fruit

125g (4oz) chopped mixed peel

grated rind of 1 orange

60ml (4 tbsp) Cointreau or other
orange-flavoured liqueur

375g (13oz) unsalted butter,
softened

375g (13oz) dark muscovado
sugar

5 eggs

450g (1lb) plain white flour

TO DECORATE
45ml (3 tbsp) apricot jam

900g (2lb) white almond paste

ivory food colouring

900g (2lb) ready-to-roll icing

1½ metres fine pearlised beading

pearl lustre dusting powder

selection of fresh flowers

1 Quarter the cherries and place in a bowl with the dried fruit, mixed peel and orange rind. Add the liqueur, stir lightly and leave to soak for several hours or overnight.

2 Grease and line a deep 25cm (10 inch) round cake tin. Preheat the oven to 140°C/275°F/gas 1. Cream the butter and sugar together in a bowl until soft and fluffy. Beat in the eggs, one at a time, adding a little of the flour to prevent curdling. Sift the remaining flour and fold in. Add the soaked fruits and stir until evenly combined. Turn the cake mixture into the tin and bake for 3½–4 hours or until a skewer inserted in the centre of the cake comes out clean. Leave to cool in the tin. Turn out and wrap in a double thickness of foil. Store in a cool place for up to 2 months.

3 To finish the cake, warm the jam and press through a sieve into a bowl. Stir in 15ml (1 tbsp) hot water. Brush the cake with the glaze and cover with almond paste (see page 18).

4 Knead a little ivory food colouring into the ready-to-roll icing. Use the icing to cover the cake. Roll small balls of icing from the trimmings, the same size as the beads. You will need about 40 of these. Leave to harden overnight.

5 Cut a strip of paper to fit the circumference and depth of the cake. Fold into 8 equal portions. Make a deep semicircle from two folded points, reaching almost to the base of the strip, and cut out through all thicknesses. Secure around the cake and transfer the curved outline onto the cake, using pin pricks.

6 Secure the beading around the cake over the pin pricks, brushing the area very lightly with water to secure. Cut a single bead and make about 5 impressions in the cake, below each garland.

7 Moisten a little dusting powder with water. Roll the balls of icing in the powder, then press into the impressions.

8 Just before the celebratory gathering, arrange fresh flowers on the cake.

CARAMEL GARLAND CAKE

Makes 12 slices
Preparation: 1 hour, plus cooling
Cooking time: 20–25 minutes
Freezing: suitable (stage 3)
530 cals per slice

6 eggs, separated

5ml (1 tsp) almond essence

225g (8oz) caster sugar

225g (8oz) ground hazelnuts or almonds

50g (2oz) fresh white fine breadcrumbs

5ml (1 tsp) baking powder

45ml (3 tbsp) lemon juice

45ml (3 tbsp) Grand Marnier or other orange-flavoured liqueur

CARAMEL
125g (4oz) granulated sugar

90ml (6 tbsp) water

CRÈME AU BEURRE
125g (4oz) granulated sugar

90ml (6 tbsp) water

3 egg yolks

250g (9oz) unsalted butter, softened

TO DECORATE
12 physalis fruit, opened

6–8 apricots, halved or quartered (optional)

150g (5oz) red grapes, in small bunches

1 Grease and line three 18cm (7 inch) round sandwich tins, preferably straight sided. Whisk the egg yolks in a large bowl with the almond essence and 200g (7oz) of the sugar until pale and thickened. Stir in the ground nuts, breadcrumbs, baking powder and lemon juice.

2 Whisk the egg whites in a clean bowl until stiff. Gradually whisk in the remaining sugar. Using a large metal spoon, fold a quarter of the egg whites into the cake mixture to lighten it, then carefully fold in the remainder.

3 Divide the mixture between the prepared tins and level the surfaces. Bake at 190°C/350°F/gas 5 for 20–25 minutes until risen and just firm. Transfer to a wire rack to cool.

4 Lightly oil two large baking sheets. To make the caramel, put the sugar and water in a small heavy-based pan and heat gently until the sugar is dissolved, then increase the heat. Bring to the boil and boil rapidly to a golden caramel. Dip the base of the pan in cold water to prevent further cooking, then immediately pour a little of the caramel onto one of the baking sheets, until it has spread to about 10cm (4 inches) in diameter.

5 Using a teaspoon, drizzle more syrup onto the baking sheet, to form eight round lacy shapes about 7.5cm (3 inches) in diameter. If the caramel hardens before you have shaped all of the decorations, reheat gently to melt. Leave for about 30 minutes until brittle.

6 To make the crème au beurre, gently heat the sugar and water in a small heavy-based pan until the sugar is dissolved. Bring to the boil and boil steadily until the syrup registers 107°C/225°F on a sugar thermometer.

7 Meanwhile, lightly beat the egg yolks in a bowl to break them up. Slowly pour the hot syrup onto the yolks, whisking well. Cream the butter in a separate bowl, then gradually beat in the syrup mixture until smooth.

8 Drizzle the cakes with the liqueur. Put the large piece of brittle caramel between sheets of greaseproof paper and crush quite finely, using a rolling pin. Mix the crushed caramel with a quarter of the crème au beurre. Use this to sandwich the cakes together on a large flat serving platter, at least 28cm (11 inches) in diameter. Using a palette knife, spread the remaining crème au beurre over the top and sides.

9 Arrange the fruits casually on the platter around the cake. Carefully lift the caramel shapes from the baking sheet, using a palette knife, and prop them between the fruits.

PASSION FRUIT AND COCONUT MERINGUE GÂTEAU

Serves 10
Preparation: 25 minutes, plus cooling
Cooking time: 1¼ hours
Freezing: not suitable
320 cals per serving

4 egg whites

225g (8oz) caster sugar

10ml (2 tsp) vanilla essence

50g (2oz) desiccated coconut

FILLING
12 passion fruit

60ml (4 tbsp) white rum

250g (9oz) Greek yogurt

300ml (½ pint) double cream

30ml (2 tbsp) icing sugar

TO DECORATE
passion fruit quarters

lychees or mango slices

toasted coconut shavings

1 Line three baking sheets with non-stick baking parchment, then draw a 23cm (9 inch) circle on each; invert the paper.

2 Whisk the egg whites in a bowl until stiff. Gradually beat in the sugar, a tablespoon at a time, beating well after each addition, until the meringue is stiff and glossy. Fold in the vanilla essence and coconut.

3 Spoon onto the marked circles, peaking the meringue around the edges. Bake at 140°C/275°F/gas 1 for about 1¼ hours until crisp, switching the baking sheets halfway through to ensure even cooking. Leave to cool.

4 Halve 8 passion fruit and scoop the pulp and seeds into a sieve over a bowl. Press the juice into the bowl and stir in the rum and yogurt. Whip the cream and icing sugar together in a bowl until just peaking, then fold in the yogurt mixture.

5 Place one meringue on a serving plate and spread with half of the cream mixture. Scoop the seeds from 2 passion fruit around the edge of the cream. Add a second meringue round, the remaining cream and scooped passion fruit. Top with the remaining meringue.

6 Decorate with passion fruit, lychees or mango slices and lightly toasted coconut shavings to serve.

ROSE WEDDING CAKE

Makes 125–150 slices
Preparation: about 6 hours, plus standing
Cooking time: about 11 hours
Freezing: not suitable
325–270 cals per serving

3 round rich fruit cakes (see page 15) of the following sizes: 15, 20 and 25cm (6, 8 and 10 inches)

TO ASSEMBLE
225g (8oz) apricot glaze
(see page 17)

2 round silver cake boards of the following sizes: 20 and 33cm (8 and 13 inch)

2.7kg (6lb) white almond paste

TO DECORATE
1.5kg (3¼lb) ready-to-roll icing

ivory food colouring

cornflour, for dusting

1.8kg (4lb) royal icing
(see page 20)

3 cream cake pillars

2 metres cream ribbon, 1cm
(½ inch) wide, for edges of boards

1 Brush the cakes with apricot glaze and cover with the almond paste, allowing 600g (1¼lb) for the small cake, 900g (2lb) for the medium cake and 1.2kg (2¾lb) for the large cake.

2 Position the large cake on the 33cm (13 inch) board and place the medium cake directly on top of it, making sure it is positioned centrally. Put the small cake on the 20cm (8 inch) board.

3 Knead sufficient ivory colouring into the ready-to-roll icing to colour it pale ivory. Reserve 225g (8oz) for the cake boards.

4 Shape the roses from the rest of the ivory icing as follows. Take a 25g (1oz) ball of icing and roll it out very thinly to a long oval, about 22cm (8½ inches) long and 6cm (2½ inches) wide. Fold in half lengthways and press the fold down gently, but without flattening it completely. Lightly dampen the unfolded edge with water. Starting at one end, roll up the icing, starting with a tight curl to represent the centre of a rose, and then loosening it as the rose becomes larger. Trim off the unfolded end of the rose so it sits neatly on the surface. Place on a sheet of greaseproof paper. Continue to make more roses in the same way, varying the weight of the icing (and the size of the oval) to make various sizes. Leave the roses on the paper overnight to dry and set firmly.

5 Dampen the edges of the cake boards and use the reserved ivory icing to cover them, trimming off the excess around the edges.

6 Colour the royal icing pale ivory and reserve 75g (3oz) for piping. Using a palette knife, spread some royal icing over the small cake until evenly covered. Smooth over with the palette knife, but don't worry about making it perfectly flat. Use the remaining royal icing to cover the other two cakes in the same way.

7 Put the reserved icing in a piping bag fitted with a medium writing nozzle. Use a casual 'scribbling' action to pipe random lines all over the small cake, then repeat on the other two cakes. Position the pillars on the middle tier. To check the pillars are not too far apart, rest the small cake on top, then remove.

8 Arrange several roses on top of the small cake, securing them with a little piped royal icing. Arrange the remaining roses on the larger cakes, trailing some of them decoratively on the sides. Before positioning roses on the sides, trim them to a shallower depth which will make them easier to secure. Support them with cocktail sticks, if necessary. Leave overnight to set. Secure ribbon round the edges of the boards to finish.

MOIST FRUIT CAKE WITH GLACÉ FRUITS

Makes 12 slices
Preparation: 20 minutes, plus cooling
Cooking time: 1–1¼ hours
Freezing: suitable (stage 2)
515 cals per slice

200g (7oz) dried apple rings

300g (10oz) mixed dried fruit

200g (7oz) molasses sugar

175g (6oz) unsalted butter, or
margarine

275ml (9fl oz) cold black tea

350g (12oz) self-raising white
flour

5ml (1 tsp) baking powder

15ml (1 tbsp) ground mixed spice

1 egg

30ml (2 tbsp) black treacle

100g (3½oz) glacé ginger pieces

TO DECORATE
60ml (4 tbsp) apricot jam

450g (1lb) mixed glacé fruits,
such as pears, plums, cherries and
pineapple

1 Preheat the oven to 160°C/325°F/gas 3. Grease and line a deep 23cm (9 inch) round cake tin. Roughly chop the apples and place in a saucepan with the other dried fruit, sugar, butter or margarine and tea. Bring to the boil, reduce the heat and simmer gently for 5 minutes. Remove from the heat and leave to cool completely.

2 Sift the flour, baking powder and mixed spice into a bowl. Add the cooled fruit mixture, egg, treacle, ginger and liquid; beat well until the ingredients are evenly combined. Turn into the prepared tin and level the surface. Bake for 1–1¼ hours, or until a skewer inserted in the centre of the cake comes out clean. Leave in the tin for 15 minutes, then transfer to a wire rack to cool.

3 To finish the cake, heat the apricot jam in a small saucepan until softened, then press through a sieve into a bowl. Brush a little of the apricot glaze over the cake.

4 Cut any larger pieces of glacé fruit into small wedges or slices. Arrange the fruits over the cake, then brush with the remaining glaze.

TOP TIP
If more convenient, the fruits can be cooked and cooled a day in advance.

VARIATION
For a more everyday fruit cake, omit the glacé fruit·topping. Instead, generously sprinkle the top of the cake with demerara sugar or decorate with whole blanched almonds before baking.

STRAWBERRY MILLE FEUILLES

Serves 6–8
Preparation: about 25 minutes, plus chilling and infusing
Cooking time: about 20 minutes
Freezing: not suitable
425–319 cals per slice

about 225g (8oz) pack chilled ready-made puff pastry

50g (2oz) raspberries

30ml (2 tbsp) redcurrant jelly

350g (12oz) strawberries, hulled and halved

150ml (5fl oz) double cream, whipped

CRÈME PÂTISSIÈRE
300ml (10fl oz) milk

1 vanilla pod, split

3 egg yolks

75g (3oz) caster sugar

30ml (2 tbsp) cornflour

15g (½oz) butter

TO DECORATE
strawberry leaves

1 Roll out the pastry to a 23 x 30cm (9 x 12 inch) rectangle. Transfer to a dampened baking tray, prick the pastry all over with a fork and chill for about 15 minutes. Bake at 220°C/425°F/gas 7 for 10–12 minutes until golden brown. Trim the edges of the rectangle, then cut widthways into three equal strips. Turn the strips over, return to the oven and bake for another 5 minutes. Cool on a wire rack.

2 To make the crème pâtissière, heat the milk with the vanilla pod in a heavy-based saucepan until almost boiling, then remove from the heat and leave to infuse for 30 minutes.

3 Whisk together the egg yolks and sugar until frothy, then whisk in the cornflour. Strain in the milk and whisk again. Return this mixture to the pan and cook over a low heat, stirring all the time, until boiling and thickened. Remove from the heat and beat in the butter. Cover the surface of the sauce with cling film and leave to cool.

4 Meanwhile, purée the raspberries in a blender and place in a saucepan with the redcurrant jelly. Place over a low heat until the jelly has melted. Leave the raspberry mixture to cool, stirring occasionally, then stir in one-third of the strawberries. When the crème pâtissière is cold, fold in the whipped double cream.

5 When ready to serve, spread the crème pâtissière over two strips of the pastry and carefully arrange half of the plain strawberries on top of each. Lay one strip on top of the other, then top with the final layer of pastry and spoon the fruit mixture on top to cover the pastry. Serve at once, decorated with strawberry leaves.

HAZELNUT VACHERIN WITH APRICOTS

Serves 6
Preparation: about 25 minutes, plus cooling
Cooking time: about 1¼ hours
Freezing: not suitable
300 cals per slice

115g (4oz) hazelnuts

3 egg whites

175g (6oz) caster sugar

5ml (½ tsp) vanilla essence

50g (2oz) sugar

150ml (5fl oz) water

225g (8oz) fresh apricots, halved and stoned

grated rind of 1 lemon

150ml (5fl oz) double cream

sprigs of mint and fresh apricots, to decorate

1 Spread out the hazelnuts on a baking tray and grill, shaking frequently, until browned. Leave to cool completely, then finely chop with a sharp knife. (Do not chop the hazelnuts in the food processor as this will make the meringue too oily.)

2 Whisk the egg whites until holding soft peaks, then whisk in half of the caster sugar, a spoonful at a time. Whisk for about 30 seconds until holding quite stiff peaks, then fold in the remaining caster sugar. Carefully fold in the hazelnuts with the vanilla essence.

3 Spoon the mixture into a large piping bag fitted with a 0.6cm (¼ inch) plain nozzle. Line two baking trays with non-stick baking parchment and draw a 23cm (9 inch) circle on each. Pipe the meringue in a spiral to make a complete round on each piece of paper.

4 Bake the meringue in the oven at 150°C/300°F/gas 2 for 40–50 minutes until dry and crisp. Leave to cool on the baking trays, then carefully peel off the paper.

5 While the meringues are cooling, place the remaining sugar in a pan with the water and place over a low heat. Stir until the sugar has dissolved, then add the apricots and lemon rind and simmer for 10 minutes until the apricots are just tender, yet still holding their shape.

6 Remove half of the apricots from the pan and set aside. Cook the rest for 5 minutes more until very soft, then drain (reserving the syrup) and push through a sieve to remove the skins. Allow to cool.

7 When ready to serve, spread half of the apricot purée over one meringue. Whip the cream to soft peak stage and carefully spread over the apricot purée. Arrange the reserved apricot halves on the cream, and place the remaining meringue round on top. Stir 45ml (3 tbsp) of the reserved syrup as a sauce with the vacherin. Decorate with mint and slices of fresh apricot.

SPECIAL CELEBRATION CAKE

Makes 30 slices
Preparation: 1½ hours, plus standing
Cooking time: about 1 hour
275 cals per slice

Madeira cake mixture made with 275g (10oz) flour and flavoured with lemon juice and rind (see page 12)

FILLING
175g (6oz) unsalted butter, softened

250g (9oz) icing sugar

60ml (4 tbsp) brandy

TO DECORATE
1.5kg (3¼lb) ready-made white almond paste

cornflour, for dusting

1.8kg (4lb) ready-to-roll icing

yellow food colouring

ICING RIBBONS
400g (14oz) icing sugar

100g (3½oz) cornflour

90ml (3½fl oz) water

20g (4 tsp) powdered gelatine

5ml (1 tsp) cream of tartar

a little egg white, beaten

a little sunflower oil

gold dusting powder

icing sugar, for dusting

TO FINISH
1.5 metres gold and white cord or ribbon

1 Grease and line a 25cm (10 inch) square cake tin. Turn the cake mixture into the prepared tin and bake at 170°C/325°F/gas 3 until firm. Leave to cool in the tin, then turn out onto a wire rack and leave until cold.

2 For the filling, beat the butter and icing sugar together in a bowl until pale and creamy. Beat in the brandy. Halve the cake horizontally. Reserve 90ml (6 tbsp) of the butter cream and use the remainder to sandwich the cakes together. Spread the remainder thinly over the top and sides of the cake. Place the cake on the board and cover with almond paste (see page 18). Reserve 150g (5oz) of the icing; colour the remainder pale yellow. Roll out the yellow icing and cover the cake. Leave in a cool place overnight.

3 To make the ribbon decoration, mix the icing sugar and cornflour together in a bowl. Put the water in a small heatproof bowl and sprinkle on the gelatine and cream of tartar. Leave to stand for 5 minutes, then place the bowl in a pan of simmering water until the gelatine is dissolved. Add to the icing sugar mixture and beat well to form a smooth paste. Turn out onto a surface dusted with icing sugar and work in a little extra icing sugar until the dough is smooth, firm and no longer sticky. Wrap in cling film until ready to use. Dampen the top edges of the cake board. Roll out the white icing and use to cover the board. Trim off any excess.

4 Roll out half the ribbon icing as thinly as possible on a surface dusted with cornflour. Cut out two strips, each 6cm (2½ inches) wide and 38cm (15 inches) long. Lightly brush the cake with egg white where the two ribbons are to be positioned, then arrange the strips, crossing them over on top of the cake and trimming off any excess.

5 For the bow, thinly roll out more icing and cut out a 17 x 6cm (6½ x 2½ inch) strip. Brush one end lightly with egg white then fold over the other end and pinch together to form a loop. Use crumpled kitchen paper to hold the loop in shape until firm. Make a second loop in the same way. Make two ribbon ends from more strips and lay them over a rolling pin so they set in a curved shape. Leave to dry overnight. Gently secure the bow ends on the ribbon with a little egg white. Lay the loops over the ribbon ends. Roll a 7.5 x 5cm (3 x 2 inch) rectangle of the icing and secure it between the loops to form the knot.

6 Using a fine paintbrush, lightly brush the edges of the ribbon with oil, then brush on a little gold dusting powder, smudging it in gently. Secure

INDEX